STATISTICS WITHOUT MATHEMATICS

SAGE was founded in 1965 by Sara Miller McCune to support the dissemination of usable knowledge by publishing innovative and high-quality research and teaching content. Today, we publish more than 850 journals, including those of more than 300 learned societies, more than 800 new books per year, and a growing range of library products including archives, data, case studies, reports, and video. SAGE remains majority-owned by our founder, and after Sara's lifetime will become owned by a charitable trust that secures our continued independence.

Los Angeles | London | New Delhi | Singapore | Washington DC

DAVID J BARTHOLOMEW

STATISTICS WITHOUT MATHEMATICS

Los Angeles | London | New Delhi
Singapore | Washington DC

Los Angeles | London | New Delhi
Singapore | Washington DC

SAGE Publications Ltd
1 Oliver's Yard
55 City Road
London EC1Y 1SP

SAGE Publications Inc.
2455 Teller Road
Thousand Oaks, California 91320

SAGE Publications India Pvt Ltd
B 1/I 1 Mohan Cooperative Industrial Area
Mathura Road
New Delhi 110 044

SAGE Publications Asia-Pacific Pte Ltd
3 Church Street
#10-04 Samsung Hub
Singapore 049483

Editor: Jai Seaman
Assistant editor: James Piper
Production editor: Victoria Nicholas
Copyeditor: Richard Leigh
Proofreader: Andy Baxter
Indexer: David Rudeforth
Marketing manager: Sally Ransom
Cover design: Shaun Mercier
Typeset by: C&M Digitals (P) Ltd, Chennai, India
Printed in India at Replika Press Pvt Ltd

Library of Congress Control Number: 2015931451

British Library Cataloguing in Publication data

A catalogue record for this book is available from
the British Library

ISBN 978-1-4739-0244-2
ISBN 978-1-4739-0245-9 (pbk)

At SAGE we take sustainability seriously. Most of our products are printed in the UK using FSC papers and boards.
When we print overseas we ensure sustainable papers are used as measured by the Egmont grading system.
We undertake an annual audit to monitor our sustainability.

CONTENTS

About the Author   ix
Preface   xi
Acknowledgements   xv

0 **Before We Begin**   1

   Role of Mathematics in Statistics   1
   Numbers   3
   Variation   4
   Measurement   4
   Origins of Statistics   7
   In Conclusion   8

1 **Picturing Variability**   9

   Introduction   9
   Picturing Variation   10
   Other Ways of Picturing Variability   20

2 **Interpreting Variability**   23

   Introduction   23
   Adding and Differencing   26
   Other Transformations (Shifting, Stretching
      and Squeezing)   30

3 **Three Standard Distributions**   35

   Introduction   35
   The Uniform Distribution   36
   The Exponential Distribution   37
   The Normal Distribution   42

4 **Summarising Variation**   47

   Introduction   47
   Measuring Location   48

Measuring Spread (or Dispersion)   50
Standard Deviation and the Normal Distribution   53
Other Summary Measures of a Distribution   54

5 The Analysis of Variation   55

Introduction   55
The Archetypal Problem   57
Comparison of Several Groups   59
Quantitative Reasons for Variation   62
The Essential Idea   64
The Analysis of Variance   64

6 Covariation   69

Introduction   69
Measurement of Covariance and Correlation   74
Principle of Least Squares   77

7 Sampling   81

Introduction   81
Drawing a Simple Random Sample   84
Other Random Sampling Methods   85
Drawing Samples from a Distribution   86

8 Introduction to the Ideas of Inference   89

Introduction   89
The Essence of the Testing Problem   90
A Second Kind of Inference   94

9 Sampling Distributions and More on Inference   97

Introduction   97
Sampling Distribution of the Average   99
Sampling Distribution of the Variance   103
Note on the Determination of Sampling
   Distributions   105
Inference Continued   105
Non-Normal Sampling Distributions   108

10 Inference about Averages   111

Introduction   111
Inference from a Single Sample   112

Comparison of Two Samples   115
More than Two Samples   116
The Assumptions   119
Power   121

11 Binary Data   123

Introduction   123
The Binomial Distribution   124
Rare Events   127
Durations   130
Relationship between Binary Variables   132

12 Goodness of Fit   135

Introduction   135
The Sampling Distribution   138
Goodness of Fit of a Normal Distribution   141
The 2 × 2 Table   144

13 Unobserved Variables   147

Introduction   147
The 'Spurious Correlation' Approach   148
The Index Approach   149
The Inheritance of Intelligence: Nature versus
    Nurture   154
Latent Variables in Social Science   155

14 Retrospect   157

Review   157
Further Reading   164

Appendix   167
Index   171

ABOUT THE AUTHOR

David Bartholomew was born in England in 1931. After undergraduate and postgraduate study at University College London, specialising in Statistics, he worked for two years in the operational research branch of the National Coal Board. In 1957 he began his academic career at the University of Keele and then moved to the University College of Wales, Aberystwyth as lecturer, then senior lecturer in Statistics. This was followed by appointment to the chair in Statistics at the University of Kent in 1967. Six years later he moved to the London School of Economics as professor of Statistics where he stayed until his retirement in 1996. During his time at the LSE he also served as pro-director for three years. He is a Fellow of the British Academy, a Member of the International Statistical Institute, a Fellow of the Institute of Mathematical Statistics and has served as Honorary Secretary, Treasurer and President of the Royal Statistical Society. He has a long-standing interest in, and experience of, teaching elementary Statistics to social scientists. An early, and rather different approach was written up, with Eryl Bassett, in a Pelican book entitled *Let's Look at the Figures*, in 1971.

He has authored, co-authored or edited about 20 books and over 130 research papers and articles, many of them in the field of social Statistics broadly interpreted.

PREFACE

This is a book about the ideas of Statistics, not the methods. It was born out of the author's belief that the ideas of Statistics are not essentially mathematical in character. This view owes nothing to the apparent fact that any sign of mathematics strikes fear into the intended audience. It goes much deeper into the conceptual framework within which the subject is approached.

This book is not simply a translation of a standard textbook in elementary Statistics into a symbol-free text. Although most of the topics covered in elementary texts will be found somewhere here, readers may quickly become disorientated if they set out with this expectation. One main difference is in the rate at which topics are introduced. To the reader with some prior acquaintance with the subject it may seem that the rate of progress is very slow to begin with. This is a consequence of our concern with ideas rather than methods. The central idea is that of the frequency distribution. In fact, as far as this book is concerned, it may seem to be the only main idea. For this reason we tackle the subject from several angles. Most current textbooks pass over basic ideas of variation quite quickly in order to move on to various ways of summarising distributions without it always being clear that that is why they are doing this. The other objective, to which they move as fast as possible, is inference, particularly tests of significance. These too depend on making judgements about distributions. It therefore pays a double dividend if the reader has been well grounded in the ideas of variation and its measurement.

Elementary books and courses typically focus on how to handle well-defined problems. Too little attention is paid to motivation. That is, students get very little guidance on how the problem arises in the first place and why one should approach it in the recommended way. In an attempt to redress the balance, greater emphasis is placed here on the intuitive thinking behind standard procedures, with an emphasis on informal reasoning. To the more experienced reader this may appear somewhat tedious or even repetitive, but it is an aspect of learning which is commonly neglected. The book concludes, in Chapter 14, by making a link back to the more traditional treatments.

The book is intended to complement, not replace, the more traditional treatments on which most introductory courses for social scientists are based. Those pursuing such courses could read it before or afterwards. Read beforehand, it should make the path easier by providing a rationale for procedures which, when they are first met, often seem rather arbitrary and esoteric; read afterwards, it might provide the overall illumination which is so often lacking. Those who contemplate reading it alongside a traditional course should be aware that that the order of topics and the pace of treatment will sometimes be very different.

There are many social scientists, among others, who will never need to carry out statistical procedures themselves but will need to appreciate what others have done. This book will also provide them with a means of access so that less has to be taken on trust. It may also be useful for a general readership, including statisticians, if they should chance to come across it.

This should not be mistaken for a 'Statistics made easy' book. Whether or not readers find it easy will depend on their assessment of the intrinsic difficulty of the basic ideas. Indeed, since, in the past, much of statistical methodology has typically been learnt by rote in order to pass examinations, some may find an introduction to the raw ideas themselves a strange experience. The reader familiar with existing texts may also feel somewhat disoriented by what may sometimes appear as a strange imbalance of emphasis.

All of the technical material, so far as it appears at all, is conveyed by diagrams and, particularly, by histograms. All of these were produced using the R language, but the programs and all the details lie behind the scenes. There is a short appendix which gives an outline and some examples, but this is not an essential part of the exposition and the reader will be none the worse for ignoring it.

I have taught introductory courses in Statistics of a more traditional kind beginning at the University of Keele as long ago as the late 1950s, and including a basic introductory course at the London School of Economics at the end of the 1970s and in the early 1980s, and another at Goldsmiths, University of London more recently. I have also had the opportunity to observe the efforts of colleagues over a longer period and my impression, almost regardless of time and teacher, is that the main obstacle is the mathematics. Furthermore, this obstacle is not only in what is traditionally understood as mathematics but also in the symbolism which often seems inseparable from it.

The style is fairly informal, without being colloquial, and, in large measure, it draws on examples which are part of common experience.

As far as possible, illustrations and analogies are taken from everyday life and technical jargon is avoided as much as possible. This may sometimes have introduced an impression of imprecision, but this is inevitable when we have deliberately dispensed with the language of precision, namely mathematics. In compensation, the essentially arbitrary character of much statistical reasoning may come across more clearly.

There are no exercises, because the purpose of this book is not to prepare students for examinations or to develop a facility for carrying out statistical procedures. These aspects are better covered in more traditional texts and under the guidance of a teacher. There is, however, ample scope for repeating, or amplifying, the material given, especially by those with a basic knowledge of a computer language like R. Everything done here uses fairly simple ideas, but it is the capacity and speed of modern desktop computers which makes individual forays into the background material possible. There is no list of references, but some guidance on further reading is included in Chapter 14.

ACKNOWLEDGEMENTS

Writing this book has largely been a solo effort, but my inevitable indebtedness to others will be clearly evident. The period of gestation has lasted many years. Various colleagues and friends, too numerous to mention by name, have kindly read draft chapters and many students have unwittingly contributed as guinea-pigs by attending courses I have given. The student mentioned in Chapter 0 was, if I remember correctly, Pat Heneage, but her contribution was certainly unconscious and is perhaps long forgotten. Professor Fiona Steele of the London School of Economics has read and commented on most of the text. Professor Aglaia Kalamatianou of Panteion University of Social and Political Science, Athens, enlisted the help of some of her students to assess the likely reaction of the intended readership. I was introduced to R by Mike Allerhand of the University of Edinburgh, and he has since come to my rescue on several occasions. To them all, and especially my wife Marian, I owe a particular debt, as do all the readers of this book.

0

BEFORE WE BEGIN

Summary

This book aims to present the basic ideas of Statistics without using the language of mathematics, which is the normal medium for that purpose. The chapter therefore begins by explaining the relationship between Statistics and mathematics and goes on to introduce the key notions of number, variation and measurement. It concludes with a brief outline of the origins of the subject.

This chapter is not an essential part of the main book but is intended to prepare the reader for what follows.

Role of Mathematics in Statistics

There is a widespread belief that Statistics is necessarily mathematical and, therefore, difficult. This book aims to show that the key ideas of Statistics can be expressed without any use of mathematical symbolism at all. This is not the same as saying that one can be a statistician without a good command of mathematics; merely that one can understand what the subject is all about without a knowledge of mathematics. It must be realised that mathematical language, in which introductions are usually expressed, is both precise and concise – indeed, these are among its principal advantages. When both are dispensed with there is, necessarily, the risk of imprecision and a certain vagueness. This is something we shall have to learn to live with, but its ill effects are minimised if we concentrate on ideas – as we shall do.

The book is aimed particularly at students of social science who are required to take a Statistics course as part of their degree course and who find the mathematical aspect completely off-putting. Even if such courses are disguised under beguiling titles such as 'quantitative methods' or 'research methods', closer examination will quickly reveal that there is some statistical content which will not lose its capacity to instil fear in spite of all assurances to the contrary.

This book is certainly not intended as a substitute for those standard texts which the student will meet – quite the opposite. Once the basic ideas have been grasped, the student will be better prepared to move on to the more serious treatments. I recall, many years ago, carrying out an experiment when I first encountered mathematical resistance among students. I sat down with one student and went very slowly through the ideas until she had grasped what it was all about. This took a great deal of time and it would not have been practicable to repeat the experiment with others, or with this student a second time. I still remember her remark at the end of it all: 'Is that all there is to it?' It was indeed all there was to it, and the same could be said of most other parts of the course. The basic reason for her difficulty was that she did not appreciate that most of the ideas were already very familiar from everyday experience and could be classed as what we often call common sense.

Something which is common to all expositions of Statistics, whether mathematical or not, is the sequential character of the subject. In a subject like geography, where one might be reading a book on industrial towns, the order of chapters might not matter too much. One could dip in here and there according to one's interest and still obtain some benefit. But with introductory Statistics it is different. What comes later often depends in a crucial fashion on what has gone before. Missing a chapter or lecture effectively derails the whole enterprise. The particular advantage of a book over a course of lectures is that one can retrace one's steps and make sure that each step has been properly digested before moving on.

Arithmetic occupies, perhaps, a half-way position between the mathematical and the non-mathematical as regards its capacity to deter students. Arithmetic deals with numbers and the particular rather than the general. As far as possible, arithmetic will also be avoided, but there are occasions where the benefits seem to outweigh the disadvantages. This will occur particularly when we come to think about summary measures in Chapter 4.

One frequently meets the term *mathematical Statistics*. Strictly speaking, this is a branch of mathematics centred on the proof of theorems starting from well-specified axioms. It bears much the same relationship to practical Statistics as does geometry to surveying and architecture. Geometry belongs to an idealised world, but one which is sufficiently close to the real world for many of its results to be transferable. The fit is perhaps less close in the case of Statistics, and this means that the results of mathematical Statistics need to be applied with particular care. Applied statisticians should not be intimidated when it is pointed out that their methods are 'inadmissible' or 'biased' because these terms relate to an idealised world which may not exactly match the real world in which they are operating. One cannot, of course, suppose that the extraction of the core ideas of Statistics in a book such as this can be done without making a subtle change in the subject itself, but this is a topic for the philosophically minded which lies outside our remit.

Numbers

Statistics is about extracting meaning from numbers – especially from collections of numbers. It is therefore crucial to know something about the numbers from which everything starts and on which it depends. This aspect may be lost sight of in the body of the book, so it is worth making the point clear before we begin. The numbers with which we shall be mainly concerned here are measures of some quantity such as length, money or time. That is, they are quantities – of something. But numbers can also mean different things according to their context. The number 3, for example, could mean a variety of things according to the way it is used. It could be the rank order of a pupil in a class examination. It could be the weight in kilograms of a bag of tomatoes, and in this case it might be the actual weight or simply the weight to the nearest kilogram. It might be the time, as for example in '3 o'clock', which might be when a meeting starts. Even if it refers to a weight in kilograms, the same amount could be expressed, equivalently, in pounds or ounces. Usually all of these matters have been sorted out before statistical analysis begins, and so they are easily taken for granted. We assume that this is true for this book also. But it must never be forgotten that what we are about to do only makes sense if the collections of numbers dealt with are of the same kind. We must not mix different units of length or, more generally, mix numbers referring to different kinds of things. An important thing is to distinguish numbers which are measurements of some kind from numbers which are simply being used as codes. A good example of the latter is provided by the numbers which footballers have on the back of their shirts. These numbers may well convey a meaning which is perfectly understood by *aficionados* of the game, but they do not measure any quantitative characteristic of the players. Similarly the scoring system in tennis may seem idiosyncratic (love, 15, 30, 40, game), until it is remembered that the numbers and names are merely labels and not quantities on which we may do arithmetic.

Variation

Since we are claiming that the key idea of Statistics is *variation,* we need to note what it means to say that different kinds of number are varying. Virtually everyone has a nationality and people differ according to their nationality. We may therefore legitimately say that nationality is something which varies from one individual to another. People also differ in age and this enables us to say that age varies from one individual to another. But the variation in age differs from the variation in nationality. In the case of age, differences can be specified in quantitative terms – they measure something. In the case of nationality, the differences cannot be so specified numerically. Hence, although it makes sense to add up ages and calculate an average age, there are no numbers we can sensibly add up to form an 'average' nationality. It is true that by showing an excessive zeal for quantitative analysis some have assigned numbers to nationality in some way, but the average nationality calculated from such numbers would have no real meaning. Rather than detain the reader with formal definitions of levels of measurement, we shall proceed with this example to serve as a warning that it is important to be clear about what the numbers mean before we start on any analysis. Broadly speaking, we started by thinking of numbers as 'amounts of something', which makes it meaningful to speak of the variation between individuals in quantitative terms. Notice that ordinal numbers, which are equivalent to ranks, do not fall into this category because knowing that two individuals are ranked 7th and 13th, say, tells us nothing about how far apart they are. Is the difference between them, for example, greater or less than that between the individuals ranked 8th and 14th?

Measurement

Before going any farther we shall pause, to briefly notice some of the different sorts of number that arise in statistical work. The simplest kind of measurement is a *count*. Many measurements that we encounter are counts. The number of people in a household, the population of a town and the number of eggs in a bird's nest are all counts and they have a direct and obvious meaning intelligible to everyone. Counts must be whole numbers and they cannot be negative. Because such numbers measure a quantity and vary among themselves, we are justified in including them among what we collectively call *variables*.

Next we come to the sort of measurements we make with instruments, such as a ruler or a pressure gauge. These operations also yield numbers but, unlike counts, they need not be whole numbers and their accuracy is limited only by the precision of the measuring instrument or our ability to use it. Essentially we are comparing the thing to be measured with some standard represented by the length of intervals on a ruler, for example. We normally record what we have measured to the accuracy determined by the quality of our instrument or our eyesight. More sophisticated measuring systems do not rely directly on human perception, but the principle is the same.

A fundamental feature of all such measures is that the scale of measurement is often *arbitrary*. The choice between yards, feet and inches and metres and centimetres as measures of length is a very important practical matter but it is usually of no theoretical significance. Length, time, weight and pressure are all physical quantities, but they have no *natural* scale of measurement. To them we may add money. Monetary values may be measured in dollars, rupees or pounds and although the pound, the rupee and the dollar may have great national significance, that position does not arise from anything inherent in that choice of unit. The arbitrariness of such scales is very important because the degree of variability exhibited by any quantity depends on the scale of measurement. The variation in the time taken to run a kilometre by a group of athletes yields a much larger number when expressed in milliseconds rather than in hours. If we do not want our conclusions to be equally arbitrary, the arbitrariness in the scale of such measurements must be made irrelevant for the purpose in hand. Our conclusion may be formally stated as follows. *We should not do anything with the numbers or draw any conclusions from them which depend on an irrelevant unit of measurement.* Thus the end-product of any calculations we make with money should not depend on whether we work in pounds, dollars or guilders or anything else.

The arbitrariness of the unit of measurement can be very limiting, but worse is to come! We may measure air temperature in degrees Fahrenheit or Celsius, but when we do this it is not only the scale of the unit of measurement which differs. The two scales also have different *origins*. The origin is the temperature to which we assign the value zero.

This is no problem with length or weight, for example, because we all know what is meant by a zero length or zero weight. Temperature is not quite like that. There is in fact a natural zero point which occurs when all molecules are at rest, but this is so far removed from the scale we need in meteorology, for example, that it is almost irrelevant. Absolute zero occurs when all the molecules in a piece of matter are at rest because, to a physicist, temperature is a measure of the activity of the molecules and this has a natural origin. On the Celsius scale it is at −273 degrees. Although some parts of the universe are almost as cold as that, it would be very inconvenient to measure the air temperature on our planet using such an origin because all the resulting numbers would be large and close together. Instead we choose an arbitrary origin to suit our own convenience. If we extend the principle enunciated above to cope with the new situation it becomes: *We should check whether anything we do with temperatures depends on either the unit of measurement or on the origin from which the measurements are made.*

This brings us back to ordinal measurements. As we have seen, these are rather different in that they do not attempt to place individuals on a scale in the same sense as the quantities we have just discussed. The number assigned to an individual merely tells us where that individual comes in the rank order of the set of individuals with which it is to be compared. This precludes doing any arithmetical operation on them which goes beyond their ordinal character. The natural way to assign numbers is to use the numbers 1, 2, 3, ... so that the 7th largest member has the number 7 and so on. But any other set satisfying the basic order restriction would serve as well. We could take only the odd numbers or, to take a rather bizarre example, we could use only the prime numbers, provided only that the order condition was met. Our general principle when applied to ordinal numbers, therefore, says that *we should do nothing with the ordinal numbers which makes the result depend on what particular set of labels we happen to have chosen to use.*

It should be clear, by now, that the numbers with which we have to deal are not all the same. As we have already noted, books on Statistics for social scientists sometimes speak about 'levels of measurement', and this involves a more systematic treatment of the same idea. The guiding principle underlying this discussion is that our analysis should not require more of the numbers than their level of measurement justifies. In practice it says that all our data should consist of measures of size of the same kind expressed in the same units.

There is much to be said for the idea that the early stages in education should concentrate on instilling information – even rote learning – on the grounds that illumination will follow, and cannot be had until a sufficient foundation has been absorbed. But it does not always seem to work like that with Statistics where, among the readership we have in mind, the incentive to learn the language first is entirely lacking. It therefore seems worth beginning at the other end by pointing out that much of the learning has already been done and all that one has to do additionally is to uncover it and expose its relevance.

Those already well versed in the subject may be having doubts about our assertion that some of the ideas of Statistics are already familiar, and they will claim that others are unfamiliar and counterintuitive. This may sometimes be true, especially if one tries to swallow too much at one bite; we also have to recognise that common sense is not so very common. These are problems we shall have to meet and try to solve as we go. As we have already noted, there are no exercises in this book of the usual kind, but rather we offer an invitation to look around the world and see examples of Statistics everywhere. For this reason our examples are drawn from a very wide field of common experience and not restricted to the social sciences alone.

Origins of Statistics

Although the name 'Statistics' has a long history, the name is, in effect, an Anglicisation of the German word for 'state science'. Modern Statistics can be more accurately dated from the work of Karl Pearson at University College London around 1900. Variation was in fact the key element in early Statistics, especially in the tradition stemming from Karl Pearson's predecessors, Charles Darwin and Francis Galton. Stigler, for example, makes the following remark about Darwin's *Origin of Species*:[1]

> Accordingly, chapters 1, 2 and 5 were exclusively concerned with variation, starting with variation in domestic plants and animals. Darwin developed a wealth of information on dogs, pigeons, fruit and flowers. By starting with domestic populations he could exploit his reader's knowledge of widespread experience in selective breeding and agriculture to improve the breed and the crop. The substantial variation was convincingly argued and, what's more, the variations that he presented were demonstrably heritable.

[1] Stigler, S.M. (2010) Darwin, Galton and the Statistical Enlightenment. *Journal of the Royal Statistical Society, Series A*, 173, 469–82.

The early volumes of the journal *Biometrika,* founded and edited by Pearson, are full of frequency distributions of biological and anthropological variables. Since then there has often been a tendency to overlook or even ignore distributional matters by focusing on particular aspects of distributions such as the average. As the subject has grown, its spread has increased enormously and now hardly any branch of science – or social science – is beyond its reach.

It may seem slightly odd that in a book directed primarily to social science students, we should trace the origins of the subject to biology. Nevertheless, that is where the origins actually lie. The founding father of social Statistics in the UK in a social science context was Sir Arthur Bowley, the first professor of Statistics at the London School of Economics and Political Science, and possibly the first professor of Statistics in the world. In 1910 he published his *Elements of Statistics* which ran through many editions. Although it is devoid of any discussion of frequency distributions until Part II, and even then only briefly, Bowley makes profuse acknowledgement in the Preface of his debt to his academic neighbour Karl Pearson and his associates at University College London.

In Conclusion

It was Pierre Simon de Laplace, speaking of probability theory, who said that at bottom it was common sense reduced to calculation. We are claiming that something similar may be said of Statistics, though it might be more accurate, as far as this book is concerned, to reverse the statement and say that it is calculation reduced to common sense!

1

PICTURING VARIABILITY

Summary

Variation is a central idea in Statistics. It may be represented pictorially as a histogram or frequency curve or by numbers in a table. This chapter is designed to introduce the reader to patterns of variation which occur in the world around us and, in particular, to their pictorial representation. The ideas are illustrated by a range of examples, including sentence lengths and spam messages.

Introduction

There is one key idea which underlies most of Statistics. This is the idea of *variation*. If we make measurements of almost anything there will be variation in the results. Any doubts which the reader may have on this score should have been dispelled by the end of the next chapter. Understanding this simple fact and learning how to describe it is half the battle. Variation can be represented in several ways, but here we shall rely entirely on diagrams or pictures. Once we learn how to interpret the pattern of variation revealed by a picture we shall be able to understand the ideas which lie behind most statistical procedures.

Before proceeding, let us pause to elaborate on the key idea a little more, because the claim that *variation* is the central thing may seem radical and surprising to the unprepared reader. In many ways our whole culture, especially as seen through the media, ignores variation. What matters for them is the typical or 'average' or 'representative' case. They are continually inviting us to accept simple statements which end up with some phrase, often implied if not actually stated, such as 'other things being equal'. We all know that other things will not be equal. Things do vary – we experience that variation all the time – and so we have to get back to the reality underlying these simplifications wished on us by the media. The first – and a very important – part of the book is, therefore, taken up with looking at how things actually vary and what that variation means. Only when this idea is securely fixed shall we come to look at why they vary and only then at ways of summarising what is represented by that variation.

It might be argued that there are two basic ideas behind Statistics, not one, and the second idea is *uncertainty*. Our reason for leaving this aside, until much later in the book, is that it is little more than the first idea in a different guise. If something varies we are bound to be uncertain about what values we shall observe next. Conversely, if an outcome is uncertain there will be variation in successive values of it which occur. For if there were no uncertainty we would know exactly what to expect, and that is the same as saying that successive values will not vary! The approach via uncertainty is particularly attractive to mathematicians and accounts, perhaps, for the unattractiveness of the subject to those who find mathematics difficult. It is therefore worth seeing how far we can go without it.

Once the idea of variation is firmly fixed we can go on to look at what is known as *covariation*. This is a natural extension of the idea, and with it we move into the realm of relationships among things that vary – and come to the extremely important notions of correlation and causation.

In the second half of the book, we shall see that there may be some point in actually creating variation artificially, because it enables us to understand how to interpret the sources of real variation. This enables us to compare actual variation with what might have happened.

Picturing Variation

Let us begin with a collection of numbers. It does not much matter what they represent, but actually they are the numbers of words per sentence in the leading article of the London *Times* newspaper on 15 April 2011.

27, 23, 33, 15, 21, 38, 16, 15, 4, 19, 21, 9, 33, 41, 10, 30, 35, 19, 17, 31, 33, 17, 22, 10, 22, 29, 35

It is immediately obvious that the number of words varies considerably over the range covered, but there are no very long sentences – with more than 50 words, for example – and few that are very short. It is much easier to take in the general picture if we arrange them in order as follows:

4, 9, 10, 10, 15, 15, 16, 17, 17, 19, 19, 21, 21, 22, 22, 23, 27, 29, 30, 31, 33, 33, 33, 35, 35, 38, 41

We can now see immediately that the numbers range from 4 to 41. This allows us to take in much more at a single glance – for example, that although the range is quite large, there seems to be quite a lot of numbers concentrated somewhere in the middle of the range.

A big step on the way to picturing the variation is to place the numbers on a scale as we have done in Figure 1.1. This enables us to see the spacing and, thus, where values are concentrated.

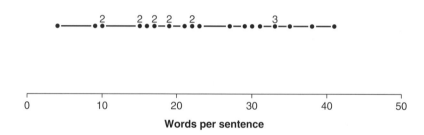

Figure 1.1 Variation of words per sentence for Times(1) data

The numbers printed above some of the dots are frequencies. For example, there were two sentences having 10 words each so a '2' appears above the dot plotted at '10 words'. Figure 1.1 confirms our impression of a concentration around 20 and another in the low 30s, and that is perhaps as far as it is worth going with such a small number of sentences. However, if we had a much larger number of sentences, say 200 or 1000, it would be very tedious to construct a diagram like Figure 1.1 and we might wonder whether there was an easier way to get an overall picture of the variation.

There is, and, paradoxically as it may seem, we can get a clearer view of the general pattern by throwing away some of the detail. And in doing this we meet one of the most important ideas of Statistics, which is that there is often a trade-off between detail and generality. In the present case we shall illustrate this even though, with such a small number of sentences, it might seem rather like 'gilding the lily'. Instead of plotting the lengths as in Figure 1.1, let us merely record how many numbers occur in successive intervals as follows. The choice of interval is somewhat arbitrary, but suppose we merely record how many sentences have lengths in the intervals 0–5, 6–10, 11–15 and so on. The result is as follows:

0–5	6–10	11–15	16–20	21–25	26–30	31–35	36–40	41–45	46–50
1	3	2	5	5	3	6	1	1	0

This is called a *frequency distribution* for the obvious reason that it tells us how the frequency of occurrence of different lengths is distributed across the range. The clustering in the low 30s and around 20 is made more obvious in this way. The final and key step is to present this information pictorially, as in Figure 1.2, in what is called a *histogram.* What we have done is to construct a series of rectangles to replace the frequencies, with the sizes of the rectangles matching the frequencies. The word 'histogram' has a classical origin referring to the height of the rectangles whose base covers the interval for which the frequency is counted.

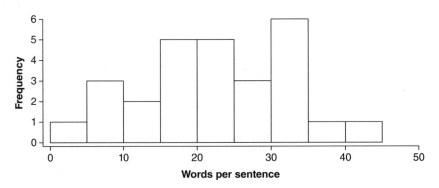

Figure 1.2   Histogram of sentence length frequency for Times(1) data

The histogram provides a *picture* of the variation in sentence length, and the whole of this book revolves around interpreting the *patterns revealed by histograms.* We note, in passing, that there is some ambiguity in this figure about the category into which a sentence length of 20, say, goes. This is an important practical matter, which is taken care of automatically by R, but it need not detain us here, and subsequently, because we are concerned with the overall shape of the distribution which is not significantly affected.

   In order to fix the idea behind this example and to see, incidentally, that patterns of variation may themselves vary, we shall repeat the same exercise using the sentence lengths in the second leading article in the same newspaper on the same day. There are rather more sentences in this case and, in the order of occurrence, they were as follows:

9, 11, 16, 22, 18, 21, 11, 24, 12, 21, 5, 17, 5, 15, 15, 15, 20, 17, 13, 20, 16, 7, 38, 38, 17, 19, 23, 11, 12, 17, 9, 12, 12

It is immediately obvious that they tend to be rather shorter than in the previous article, and this fact becomes more obvious if we list them straight away in order as follows:

5, 5, 7, 9, 9, 11, 11, 11, 12, 12, 12, 12, 13, 15, 15, 15, 16, 16, 17, 17, 17, 17, 18, 19, 20, 20, 21, 21, 22, 23, 24, 38, 38

The range is much the same as before, extending from 5 to 38 in this case, but the concentration is now between 10 and 20. This becomes even more obvious when we plot the spacings as in Figure 1.3.

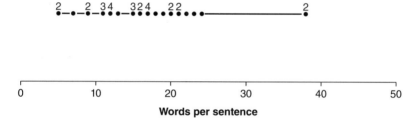

Figure 1.3 Variation of words per sentence for Times(2) data

Finally, we express the data in the form of a histogram in Figure 1.4.

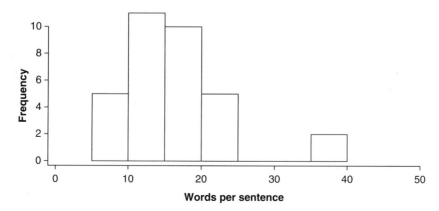

Figure 1.4 Histogram of sentence length frequency for Times(2) data

Both Figures 1.3 and 1.4 show a rather different picture for the second *Times* extract. In this case, apart from the two outliers of 38 words, there is a concentration of frequency in the neighbourhood of 15 words. This shows that the sentence lengths tend to be shorter for the second extract than for the first.

Hitherto we have been concerned with how to picture variability and we have concluded that the histogram achieves what we wanted. There are, of course, other ways of telling the same story and we shall briefly mention some of them at the end of this chapter. First, however, we look at a few other empirical distributions. This will enable us to appreciate the variety of shapes which occur in practice and it also helps us to start thinking about what lies behind these shapes. In short, we would like to know why frequency distributions take on the shape that they do. This leads naturally to the question of what we can infer from the shape of the distribution about the mechanism by which it was generated.

Our first example actually consists of two distributions. They were collected from my own computer, and the reader may care to collect distributions in a similar way. A great deal of traffic on the Internet consists of what is called 'spam'. Spam messages are sent out in bulk by advertisers of one sort or another to many computers and are usually of no interest whatsoever to the recipient. To save the time and effort of looking at all these messages, computers are usually provided with 'spam filters' whose purpose is to extract what is judged to be spam and place it in a 'bin' where it can be quickly scanned by the recipient before deletion.

The number of spam messages varies from day to day. What is the pattern of such variability? To answer this question I collected the daily numbers of spam messages for about a month early in 2013, and later in the year I repeated the exercise for a similar period. Histograms for the two periods are given in Figure 1.5.

Two things about this figure are quite striking. First, the shape of the histogram at the top is very much like that which we found for the word length distribution in Figure 1.2, yet the subject matters are totally different. This raises the hope that there may be a few commonly occurring shapes; if so, it might greatly simplify the matter of interpretation of frequency distributions. Secondly, the histograms in the two parts of Figure 1.5 are quite different even though they refer to the same thing (spam messages). One immediately wonders why there should be this striking difference. There is in fact a good explanation for this difference, but the curious reader will have to wait until Chapter 2 to find out what it is. Note that the vertical scales of frequency are not the same in the two cases. This is because the scales have been arranged to make the histograms about the same size. Size does not matter here because it is the 'shapes' that we are comparing.

We now turn to two distributions which show, among other things, that the shapes already observed by no means exhaust the possibilities.

Unlike the earlier examples, the distribution in Figure 1.6 has a high concentration of frequencies at the beginning, and these tail away rapidly with one extreme value just short of 600 seconds.

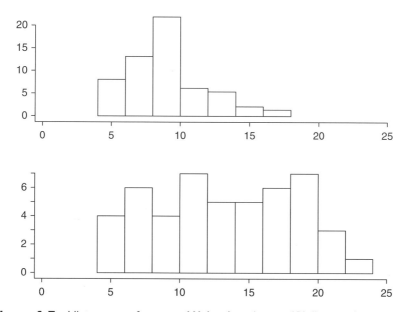

Figure 1.5 Histograms for spam(1) (top) and spam(2) (bottom)

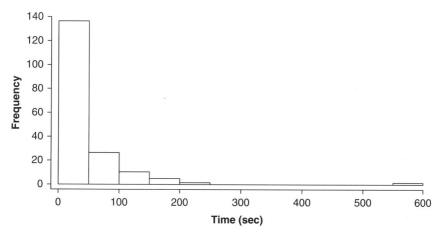

Figure 1.6 Time intervals (seconds) between passing vehicles

The second distribution (Figure 1.7) is somewhat similar in shape but arises in a totally different way, and one does not need to know the exact meaning of 'nearest neighbour' to appreciate this.

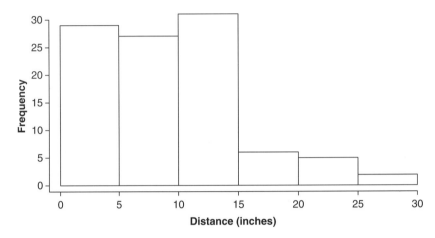

Figure 1.7   Histogram of nearest neighbour distances for seedlings

Figure 1.7 may seem a rather odd choice as an example because it concerns the distribution in space of seedlings growing in the vicinity of sycamore trees. Its interest for us is twofold. Spatial distributions are very important in social science, but real examples are so hedged about with qualifications that it has proved very difficult to find examples to illustrate the point we wish to make at the present elementary level. Furthermore, there is a certain arbitrariness about what we have chosen to measure, and this prepares the ground for a further discussion of this example in the next chapter. Looking at the distribution in Figure 1.7, we notice that it is heavily skewed to the smaller distances but it is not so extreme as the traffic data of Figure 1.6. For the moment we simply note that it forms an interesting addition to the collection of distributions we have met so far.

Our final example may also seem rather strange because it is derived from a source which may well be unfamiliar to most readers. It concerns the distribution of random numbers, the very name of which involves the concept of randomness which will not arise until the later part of this book. The reader must therefore accept, for the moment, that such numbers play a central role in Statistics and that it is useful to know something about their distribution. Imagine that all numbers between 0 and 99 are recorded on slips of paper or on balls and then put into a lottery. Balls are drawn in the manner of a lottery and the number on each is recorded before being returned. We could then construct a frequency distribution of the numbers drawn in the usual way. Figure 1.8 provides the resulting frequency distribution for 200 numbers drawn in a fashion equivalent to that which we have just described.

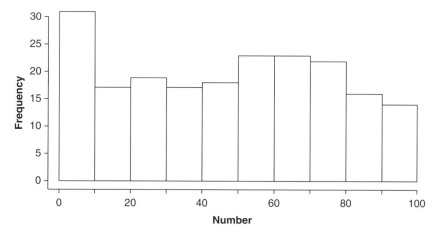

Figure 1.8 Histogram of 200 random numbers between 0 and 99

The histogram has been constructed so that each number group includes ten successive numbers 0–9, 10–19 and so on. We might have guessed that the frequency in each group would be around 20 because the 200 numbers should be evenly distributed. On average that is roughly true, but the actual frequencies range from 15 to 33. These discrepancies raise questions which we cannot answer at the moment, but the main point to notice at this stage is that the broad shape of the distribution is unlike any we have met so far. There is no tendency to level off at the ends and there is no clear peak. It is, in fact, fairly uniform.

These remarks lead us to reflect on the way that we have been using the word 'shape' in the present chapter. When describing the various histograms we might speak of 'having a hump' or 'tailing off' at the ends. In doing this we have, perhaps unconsciously, been 'smoothing out' the ups and downs and imagining a broad underlying pattern. This, in fact, is a characteristic feature of statistical thinking. We are looking for broad patterns which appear to be more 'fundamental', in some not very precisely defined sense.

Coming back to the idea of a frequency distribution, we might won-der whether, if we took a much larger number of random numbers, the irregularities we observed in Figure 1.8 might be 'ironed out' to some extent. This can be investigated empirically by taking a much larger col-lection of random numbers and seeing what effect this has on the shape of the histogram. The results of one such trial are given in Figure 1.9.

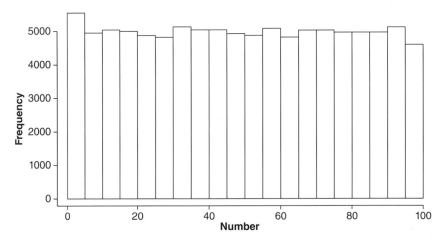

Figure 1.9   Histogram of 100,000 random numbers between 0 and 99

The distribution now appears much more 'uniform', which is a name we might justifiably give to the shape of this distribution.

It seems reasonable to conjecture that patterns might, usually at least, conform to a smooth outline if only we take a large enough number of observations. There are good reasons for this expectation, as we shall see later, but before leaving the matter for the time being, we shall give one example of a histogram whose outline does conform quite closely to a smooth curve.

The data set relating to intervals between traffic was only one of six such sets. The histogram for the distribution in the combined data set is given in Figure 1.10. A fairly fine grouping has been chosen in this case, and although the outline is still somewhat jagged, especially at the upper end, it is, nevertheless suggestive of a fairly smooth declining curve. This point is made even more clearly if we compare this histogram with Figure 1.11, which uses the same grouping intervals to show the data of Figure 1.6.

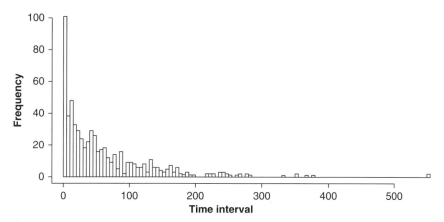

Figure 1.10 Combined distributions for intervals between vehicles

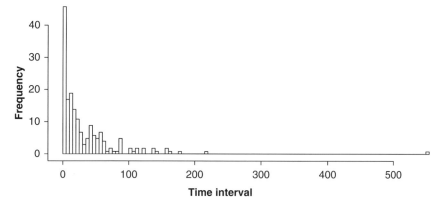

Figure 1.11 Distribution of intervals between vehicles: data of Figure 1.6 with 100 intervals

Roughly speaking, it appears that the larger the data set the easier it will be to describe the outline by reference to a curve with a simple shape. So far, at least, this is a purely empirical observation and there is no reason to expect that this will always or necessarily be the case. However, it will be convenient to get into the habit of imagining the histogram to be approximated by a smooth curve whose shape can be simply described. For example, and it is a very simple example, the distribution of Figure 1.8 may be described as a rectangle. The general name used for such a curve is the *frequency curve*. In later chapters it will often be more convenient to talk about frequency curves rather than histograms, and many of the diagrams given there will show such curves because it is easier to comprehend the message in that way. Nothing more is implied, we emphasise again, than would be conveyed by the equivalent histograms.

Other Ways of Picturing Variability

There are other ways of picturing variability, some of which we shall briefly describe, but none is as widely useful, for our purposes, as the histogram.

The *frequency polygon* is little more than a histogram in another guise. It may be obtained from the histogram by drawing lines connecting the mid-points of the tops of the rectangles which form the histogram. This has the effect of smoothing out the edges of the histogram, thus making it more closely resemble what we have called the frequency curve. The choice between the two is largely a matter of taste, but we prefer the histogram because it can be so easily constructed by any statistical software – especially R which has been used in this book.

The *cumulative frequency distribution* is equivalent to the frequency distribution in the sense that it conveys the same information in a different form. For our purposes this is less good at giving a visual picture of the variation. Instead of listing the individual frequencies, we add them up in a fashion which is best explained by an example. We use the first frequency distribution on sentence length given at the beginning of the chapter. This was set out as in Table 1.1.

Table 1.1 Frequency distribution and cumulative frequency distribution of Times(1) data

	0–5	6–10	11–15	16–20	21–25	26–30	31–35	36–40	41–45	46–50
Frequency	1	3	2	5	5	3	6	1	1	0
Cumulative frequency	1	4	6	11	16	19	26	27	28	28

Each number in the last row is obtained by adding the frequency in the top line to the number immediately to its left. The number 19 for the 26–30 group is thus the cumulative frequency up to and including that group – and similarly for the other entries. We can plot each cumulative frequency against the upper boundary of its associated group. Thus 19 is the number of sentence lengths which have lengths less than or equal to 30. The result of doing this is the cumulative frequency distribution. It does not convey information about the pattern of variability as conveniently as the histogram, as the reader may readily verify by constructing cumulative frequency distributions for some of the data sets used in this chapter.

There is nothing special about adding up frequencies from the left-hand side. It could be done just as well from the right. In some applications, where the variable is a life time, the result of doing this is known as the *survival curve* for obvious reasons.

The *boxplot* can be thought of as a summarisation of the frequency distribution. When describing such distributions we have commented on where the bulk of the frequency is located and said something about the range. The boxplot extracts such information and presents it pictorially as in Figure 1.12.

The 'box' in the centre spans the region where the middle half of the frequency is located. The bold horizontal line marks the centre and the extremes are marked by the horizontal lines connected by dotted lines. The boxplot conveys, pictorially, a good deal of the information contained in the complete distribution, but it cannot compete with the frequency distribution as far as the treatment of this book is concerned.

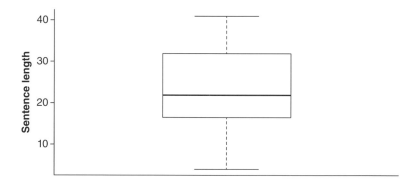

Figure 1.12 Boxplot for Times(1) data

There are other ways of presenting a picture of variability, of which the *stem and leaf* plot is one example, but this is, essentially, a kind of histogram.

2

INTERPRETING VARIABILITY

Summary

The next step is to understand why distributions have particular shapes. Clues are provided by knowing how various operations change shape. Mixing distributions is one such operation, adding or subtracting variables are two others. This introduces the ideas of the location and spread of a distribution. Applications include data relating to spatial distributions.

Introduction

Statistical science, like all scientific activity, including social science, is concerned with why things are the way they are. Although we started by looking, in a fairly haphazard way it may have seemed, at variation and what it looked like, that is not an end in itself. We now want to know how the data were generated, so far as that can be deduced from the frequency distributions. Sentence lengths, for example, seem to have a frequency distribution with a single hump somewhere near the middle and with the frequencies tailing off as we move to the extremes. But why are they that shape? Is there something about the structure of the language itself, or does the reason lie in the subject matter of the article or in the writer? We can immediately think of ways of beginning to answer such questions by looking, for example, at different specimens written by the same author or by looking at writings in different languages. 'Stylometrics' is the name given to the analysis of literary texts by statistical methods such as these, but we shall not pursue the matter here.

We shall, however, learn something about what one can deduce from the form of the frequency distribution.

There is also a different, but closely related, kind of question waiting for investigation. Often we are not really interested in the form of the distribution itself but in whether two or more distributions differ in some relevant respect. To answer such questions we shall need to look more closely at differences between distributions.

In one way or another, questions such as these underlie almost everything in this book and, indeed, the whole of the subject of Statistics. We start with an example about which we can ask questions relating both to what determines the shape of a distribution and what determines the differences between distributions. This involves knowing something about how distributions come about. We shall take this in easy stages, starting with the example of computer spam which lies behind the distributions pictured in Figure 1.5. Both distributions display similar characteristics. There is an interval over which most observations occur, and the number tails off at both extremes. But there is a striking difference between the two distributions. The second extends over a much wider range – roughly double that of the first. Since spam messages originate, one supposes, from a multitude of different sources, there is no reason to suppose that there is any collusion between senders. The number received per day should therefore be roughly the same. But this does not account for the fact that there is a much larger number in the second period. This strongly suggests that the number of sources must have increased during this time. The collection of these data was not made in anticipation of such a result and no careful watch was made of the composition of the daily tally. Nonetheless, I did notice that many of the spam messages in the second period included a proportion written in Chinese characters. This suggests that some new source of messages from the Far East was getting through and being allocated to the spam bin. If that was the case, what we are observing in the second period is an amalgamation of two streams of such messages. This fact was immediately obvious from the histograms, and the example illustrates how histograms can tell us something about 'what is going on'. What we see in the second case is therefore some sort of combination of the two distributions we would have obtained by observing the two streams separately.

This observation gives a clue as to the way in which we might begin to explain how some distributions, at least, might arise. They might be composed by combining simpler distributions in some way. In the spam example it is not difficult to see how this might have happened.

What we were, in fact, observing each day was the sum of the 'English' and the 'Far Eastern' spam messages. The observed histogram thus resulted from adding two numbers, each of which might well have had a distribution not unlike that obtained in the first period. Adding two numbers is not the only way that distributions might be combined. In this chapter we shall see what kind of shapes can be produced by such combinations and thus, to some extent, we shall have 'explained' how the resulting distribution might have come about.

Two distributions might become 'mixed up' in a variety of ways, and we begin with a mixing of distributions (rather than with the observations which led to those distributions). This will show just how limited is this path to understanding, but it can sometimes be instructive.

At this point we introduce the frequency curve into the diagrams in place of the histogram because it is the shape of the overall distribution in which we are interested, not the details of the histogram itself. Figures 2.1 and 2.2 illustrate two of the possibilities.

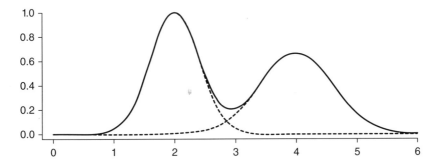

Figure 2.1 Possible mixture of two distributions

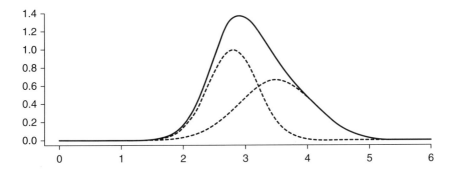

Figure 2.2 Another possible mixture of two distributions

In each case the solid line is the profile of the histogram we imagine that we have observed: the dotted lines represent two possible component distributions which, together, add up to the distribution represented by the solid curve.

In Figure 2.1 the two distinct humps strongly suggest the presence of two component distributions, but in Figure 2.2 there is no such clue because the solid curve has a shape not obviously unlike those we have already met. There is no reason to suggest that it, or any other distribution like it, is made up of two components. Indeed, we have illustrated the situation in the simplest possible case with only two components, but note that the components have been allowed to differ in average and variation. This was done only in order to make the position as clear as possible in the figures. If there were more components it would be rather unusual to find each component clearly identified by a separate hump on the distribution.

Figure 2.1 demonstrates the possibility of detecting the presence of component distributions and hence providing a partial explanation of the original picture of variability. But it also shows why heterogeneity of this kind may easily pass undetected. The idea behind this example is that a distribution may not be what it appears to be, because it may be a mixture, and we may not know this in advance. A much more important possibility is that we may have prior knowledge which leads us to expect that we are dealing with a mixture. A simple example is provided by distributions of height in human populations. If our data cover both men and women we are observing a mixture of two distributions – one for males and one for females. If we were to separate out the two distributions we would find that they were different, with women on the whole being shorter. Each distribution would have its own separate peak, but these would probably not be evident from the pooled distribution. This is typical of many practical situations where there are differences between subgroups. In fact, we shall later be very much concerned with situations where we want to know whether groups do, in fact, have different distributions. However, since we shall necessarily know what these groups are in advance, there is no occasion to consider the combined distribution at all.

Adding and Differencing

The pattern of variation can be explained in many ways and the mixing of distributions, which we have just considered, is only one of them.

Another way is by adding or subtracting the variables themselves. We have already met this in the case of the number of spam messages. We speculated that, during the second period, the messages originated from two different sources, one in the Far East and one nearer home. The number that we actually counted was thus the sum of the numbers arriving from the two sources. The difference in shape between the two distributions was illustrated in Figure 1.5. The size of both groups was too small to say anything definitive about the difference in shape, except that the numbers were much larger in the second case than the first.

We now look at the same phenomenon where much larger numbers are involved. The time intervals between passing vehicles were measured over a much longer period than we used for Figure 1.6, and these were given in Figure 1.10. In all there were 612 intervals, but the last four have been omitted so that the total number is a multiple of 8. The reason for this will soon become apparent, but it does not affect the point at issue here. We formed three new data sets. The set of intervals on the first day began with the following values:

44, 87, 2, 1, 24, 4, 2, 9, 15, 1, 16, 102, 218, 32, 28, 5, 18, 24, 6, 3, 28, 69, 11, 5, 58, 12, 7, 73, 18, 16, 4, 38, 3, 1, 26, 12, 57, …

First we formed 304 consecutive pairs and added the members of the two pairs. The sequence of such pairs therefore began

131, 3, 28, 11, 16, 118, 250, 33, …

This new set of data was thus what we would have observed if we had chosen to measure the intervals between every second vehicle. The histogram for this new set is given in the top part of Figure 2.3. Next we formed pairs from this second set, obtaining 152 intervals, each of which gives the time interval between every fourth vehicle. This sequence began

134, 39, 134, 284, …

The histogram is shown in the middle part of Figure 2.3. Finally, we repeated the operation, obtaining a set of intervals between every eighth vehicle. This sequence began

173, 418, …

The histogram in this case is given in the bottom part of Figure 2.3. By comparing the three histograms we can see how the shape of the distribution changed as we increased the number of the original intervals which have been added.

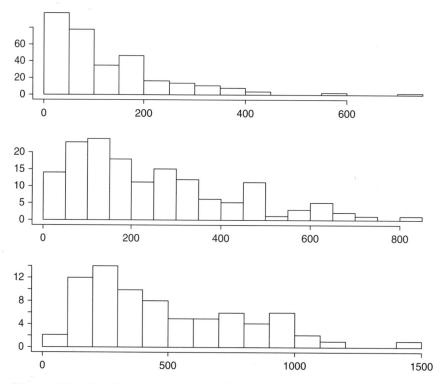

Figure 2.3 Distributions of sums of 2 (top), 4 (middle) and 8 (bottom) intervals for data used in Figure 1.10

The scales for all axes have been chosen to facilitate a comparison of the shapes of the three distributions. It appears that as we increase the number of original intervals in the partial sums added, there is a marked change in the shape. Starting with the greatest frequency at the beginning, the distribution begins to develop a 'hump' which is accentuated as we increase the number of intervals summed. By the time we have eight components in the sum the peaking of the frequencies is unmistakable. This is what intuition would suggest. The process of adding tends to 'iron out' some of the gross variation, resulting in a tendency for aggregation towards the centre. The process has not gone very far in this example because aggregating intervals in this way reduces by one half the size of the data set at each stage and its size rapidly becomes too small to show the shape reliably. Nevertheless, if we had been able to continue the process started in Figure 2.3, the change in the shape would have been even more marked.

An interesting example of how the shape of a distribution changes as we operate in different ways on an original set, is provided by differencing. This may not be of much interest in the study of traffic flow, but it introduces some new features of general practical interest. Suppose that, having created the 304 pairs in the above manner, we calculated their differences rather than their sums.

The sequence of these differences thus begins –43, 1, 20, –7, ... What would the distribution of the successive differences look like? It is instructive to bring one's intuition to bear on this before making the experiment. Given that the original intervals varied a great deal, the likelihood is that the two members of each pair will be very different in size. It is just as likely that the larger member of the pair will come first as second. Roughly speaking, therefore, every pair of the first kind will be balanced by one of the second kind, so the resulting distribution should be roughly symmetrical. Further, this will be the first distribution we have met where the variable takes negative as well as positive values. If we carry out this differencing process for the large traffic data set, we obtain the result shown in Figure 2.4.

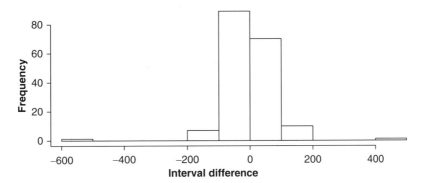

Figure 2.4 Distribution of the differences between successive intervals for the data shown in Figure 1.6

The distribution is not perfectly symmetrical, of course, but it shows that positive and negative differences are roughly balanced. We remarked earlier that such an analysis might not be of great practical interest, but the distribution does tell us something about traffic flow. What it tells us can be illustrated by asking what we would observe if vehicles were equally spaced in time. In that case all intervals would be of equal length and all the differences would be zero. The histogram would then be concentrated near zero. The more the distribution is spread out, the greater the inequality in the spacing. The dispersion shown by this distribution reflects the variability of the spacing.

Other Transformations (Shifting, Stretching and Squeezing)

Yet another way of producing one distribution from another is by trans-formation. As a first example of what is meant by this term we look again at the spacing of sycamore seedlings given in Figure 1.7. If this seems a trifle esoteric, it has the virtue of being a situation where the notion of transformation arises naturally. When observing passing traffic there is no ambiguity about what is meant by the next vehicle to pass. But, when look-ing at a spatial distribution, it is not so obvious how to measure the distance to the nearest neighbour. When reporting the data we did not raise this question but proceeded as if the distance to the nearest neighbour was the most natural way to measure distance. Another way would have been to use the area of the biggest disc, centred on one plant, which one could have drawn without touching a neighbour. This is easily obtained from the distance to the nearest neighbour because the area of the circle is calculated from what now becomes its radius. In Figure 2.5 we have given the histogram for the distribution of circle areas, which should be compared with that for 'nearest neighbour' distances given in Figure 1.7.

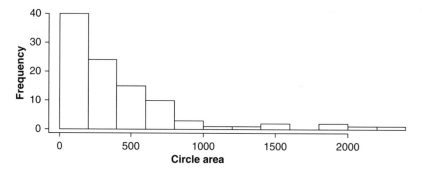

Figure 2.5   Histogram of circle sizes between sycamore seedlings

This is certainly different from the histogram of Figure 1.7, show-ing a rather greater concentration of frequency for the small intervals.

This illustrates that the variable and its distribution are closely related and that if we change one we also change the other. The shape of a distribution is therefore not fundamental because it depends on how we happen to choose to measure the variable.

The transformation from 'nearest neighbour' to 'area of free space' is quite complicated compared with some transformations which play a fundamental role in Statistics. We now turn to some of the simplest and important examples.

Essentially we are asking what happens to the distribution if we change the variable. Perhaps the simplest case is where we add the same number to each variable value. It does not require much imagination to see that the effect of this would be to shift the whole distribution by the same amount. The position is illustrated in Figure 2.6.

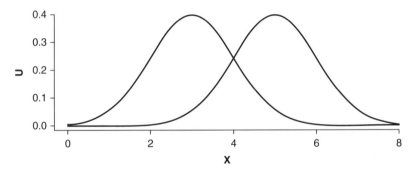

Figure 2.6 Two identical distributions, with one shifted by two units

Although this may seem a rather obvious and trivial transformation, the idea behind it underlies much of statistical practice, as we shall see in Chapter 4 and also in the later part of this book. A word of caution should be added here. The fact that it is possible to conceive of shifting a distribution bodily in this fashion does not mean that there is necessarily a good practical meaning in such a transformation. For example, although it may be conceivable that there should be a minimum non-zero time interval between passing vehicles, it is not sensible to suppose that this is possible in the state of current traffic engineering.

A second common transformation involves changing the scale of measurement. What happens, for example, if we choose to work in centimetres instead of inches? Such changes of scale involve multiplying the variable by the appropriate conversion factor. This may be thought of as a stretching, or shrinking, of the horizontal axis. The consequences of rescaling are illustrated in Figure 2.7.

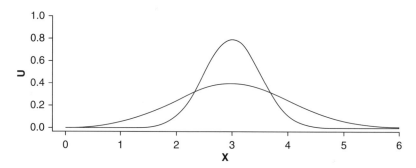

Figure 2.7 Two identical distributions, except that one has a scale double the other

It is possible, of course, to have both a shift of location and a change of scale, as illustrated in Figure 2.8.

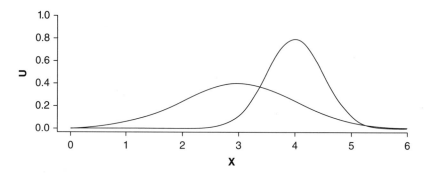

Figure 2.8 Two identical distributions, but with a shift of location and a change of scale

Such transformations are relevant where we are dealing with variables such as temperature, where there are different scales of measurement like Fahrenheit and Celsius. We can convert from a number on the Fahrenheit scale to one on the Celsius scale by subtracting 32 and multiplying the result by 5/9. In the present terminology this involves a shift in location from 32 to 0 and a change of scale effected by multiplying by 5/9.

Some transformations serve another, different purpose than those we have considered hitherto. The first we considered relating to spatial distributions arose because there were at least two ways of specifying the 'distance' between plants and we were curious to see what difference it would make to the shape of the distribution if we opted for either. Changes of scale, which we have just considered, often arise in practice. If the variable is an amount of money, for example, it ought not to matter for most purposes whether it is measured in dollars or rupees. We therefore need to know what effect the choice might have on the distributions involved so that we can make sure it does not affect the subsequent analysis. We have left to one side why it is important to know about shifts in location, but this will become clear later.

There is a further purpose in transformation which can also be important in more advanced analyses. This is because there are many more, or simpler, statistical methods available for some distributions than others. Indeed, this might lead us to wonder whether it is possible to transform any distribution into any other so that all attention could be focused on only one family of distributions. It is, in fact, possible to achieve this object by an appropriate stretching in some parts of the variable and squeezing in others. However, the question we want to answer by the analysis will also be 'transformed' in the process so that the potential advantages may be lost.

One such transformation, which can be very useful in many social science applications, arises in the study of durations. Examples are the length of time an occupier lives at a particular address and the length of time an individual spends in a job. Such variables have distributions similar to that shown in Figure 2.9 with a long tail at the upper end; a transformation can make them more tractable.

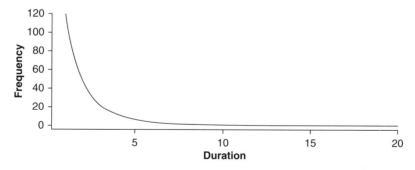

Figure 2.9 A typical distribution of a duration

It turns out that the distribution can be made almost symmetrical by working with the logarithm of duration. Readers who have met logarithms before may remember that there is something called the 'base', 10 for example. This makes no difference, for our present purposes, because its only effect is to shift the location of the transformed distribution, whereas we are only interested in its shape. One feature of the logarithmic transformation to note is that it may introduce negative numbers for the variable of the transformed distribution. We have already met such negative values in the case of differences between time intervals and noted that it makes no difference. Figure 2.10 shows the distribution of the transformed variable, and we note that the effect of the transformation is to yield a symmetrical distribution.

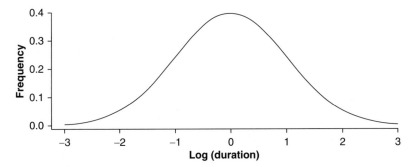

Figure 2.10 The distribution of Figure 2.9 after logarithmic transformation of duration

3

THREE STANDARD DISTRIBUTIONS

Summary

Knowing that frequency distributions have a great variety of shapes, we define in this chapter three standard distributions: the Normal, exponential and uniform, or rectangular, distributions. These distributions provide fixed points to which the shapes of other distributions can be related. They, and their associated distributions, provide a foundation for much of the rest of the book.

Introduction

We have now met enough frequency distributions to appreciate that, although they take on a variety of shapes, some seem to occur quite often in very varied circumstances. It is convenient, therefore, to pause and look at a few characteristics which seem to be common to many distributions. We shall therefore introduce what we shall call 'standard' frequency distributions. These serve three purposes. First, they are important in Statistics generally, and the reader who goes beyond this book will need to know what their names signify. Secondly, they will arise repeatedly in this book and it is useful to have a foundation of terminology on which to build. And thirdly, there is a more immediate purpose because they will serve to introduce some order into what may seem a somewhat chaotic jumble and provide points of reference for describing the shapes of distributions as they occur. Thus, for example, we shall have family names for distributions, like that in Figure 1.6, which have frequencies which decline as we move from left to right. Two of the distributions will also serve to introduce the reader to the difference between continuous and discrete distributions.

At this stage there are only three distributions to be considered, but many more exist and some of them will occur in later pages. Nevertheless, these three are enough to be going on with and they are undoubtedly important, though for different reasons. They are the uniform (or rectangular) distribution, the exponential distribution, and above all, the Normal distribution. For the most part we will continue to represent frequency distributions as curves, rather than histograms, so that we can more readily focus on their overall shape.

The Uniform Distribution

As its name implies, the *uniform* (or rectangular) distribution has a frequency distribution which has the shape of a rectangle. We have already met an example of this in connection with random numbers, and it was illustrated in Figures 1.8 and 1.9. In that case we considered the distribution of the whole numbers ranging between 0 and 99. We might have considered the whole numbers between 0 and 9 or the numbers between 0 and 1 recorded to five decimal places. In all these cases the variable in question is *discrete* because the number of possible values that it can take is limited. For example, there are 10 whole numbers between 0 and 9, and the variable must take one of them. Likewise, there are 100,000 different values for a number given to five decimal places between 0 and 1, excluding 1 itself. In this book we are concerned only with the *ideas* of Statistics, so there is little to be gained in general by drawing a distinction between discrete and continuous variables. In passing, we note that, for a discrete distribution, we could replace the histogram by what might be called a *bar diagram*. In this the frequency of occurrence of a particular variable value is represented by a column whose height is proportional to the frequency. In order to show what this might look like, an example is shown in Figure 3.1 for random whole numbers between 0 and 9.

Figure 3.1 shows the frequency of each individual whole number, rather than what we would obtain by grouping them as if they were values of a continuous variable. The histograms of Figures 1.8 and 1.9 could have been presented as bar diagrams where the variable was restricted to a fixed number of values, but little is lost, and much gained, by merging them. We shall therefore continue to make no distinction between discrete and continuous variables. The examples already discussed are not, of course, exactly rectangular in shape because they are constructed from samples, and we would only expect them to be exactly rectangular if we had a very large set of data.

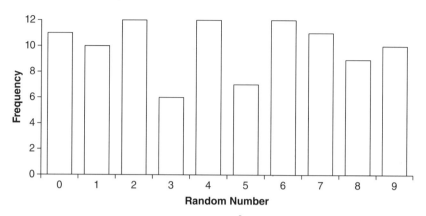

Figure 3.1 Frequency distribution of 100 random numbers, plotted as bars

Rectangular distributions may arise in other practical situations, though they are not common. For example, if we had recorded the times at which vehicles pass a given point, rather than the intervals between them, we might have found that the times were uniformly distributed throughout the period of observation – implying a constant rate of passing through the period. They are mentioned here because they are very simple in form and have a special importance in relation to random numbers whose full relevance we have yet to explore.

There is not one uniform distribution but many, because both the starting point and the end of the range may vary. The range (0,1) has a particular significance in relation to random numbers located between 0 and 1, but a distribution may be uniform over any range.

The Exponential Distribution

Many of the distributions we have encountered so far have frequencies which decrease as we move from left to right – as illustrated in Figures 1.6 and 1.10, for example. One important distribution which has this property is the *exponential* distribution. The empirical distributions shown in those figures are not in fact exponential distributions, but it is useful to refer to them as 'exponential-like' because they share a common property of decreasing frequencies. A histogram for a typical exponential distribution is given in Figure 3.2.

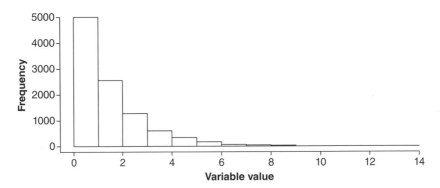

Figure 3.2   An exponential distribution

The feature of this histogram which marks it out as an exponential distribution is that each rectangle is half the height of its immediate
predecessor. It would still have been an exponential distribution if each
rectangle had been a different fraction of its predecessor – say, a third,
a tenth or any other fraction whatsoever. It is this pattern of decreasing
frequencies which distinguishes exponential distributions from all other
exponential-like distributions. Notice that all the rectangles have a base
of the same length (one unit in this example), and that is a second,
implicit, requirement. An examination of the distribution in Figure 1.6
shows that this is certainly not an exponential distribution. It is not
necessary to go beyond the first three categories to see this. Whereas the
third category is roughly half the height of the second, the second is a
much smaller fraction of the first.

The proportional decline of frequencies of the exponential distribution implies a rather remarkable property. To explain this property it
may help to adopt the terminology of a particular application.
Distributions like this often arise as durations or waiting times. For
example, the time spent waiting for an appointment or the length of
time a household lives at a particular address. Imagine that Figure 3.2
represents such a distribution and that two units of time have passed, so
we are that far into the duration. We might now ask how long we have
to wait for the next event. The distribution of such residual waiting
times will simply be that part of the histogram from the point marked 2
onwards scaled up to compensate for the removal of the waiting times
that have already occurred. This is also exponential in form. Another
way of looking at the situation is to say that this is the distribution we
would have expected to observe if we did not begin our observation

until two units of time had elapsed. However, this residual distribution has exactly the same property as did the original distribution, namely that the duration, starting at 2, is also exponential. Put more generally, it says that no matter how long we have been waiting, the distribution of the time we still have to wait is unchanged! This should not only surprise the reader but seems scarcely credible. Just what it means can be emphasised by putting the position in yet another way. Suppose that you are waiting for a letter to arrive. Then, if the distribution were really exponential, the length of time you still have to wait does not depend on how long you have already waited! This is sometimes referred to as the *memorylessness* property of the exponential distribution. Intuitively we tend to feel that if we have already waited a week the expected event ought to have come that much nearer. But that intuition is formed by jumping forward in time to the point when the interval is finally complete. Before that happens we have no idea what is going on and it would be perfectly conceivable that the longer we wait, the longer we shall have to wait, because we originally misjudged the nature of the termination process. Whatever the true situation, the exponential distribution will only occur when past experience is no guide at all to what is going to happen.

Even if exponential distributions only occur in rather special circumstances, it may be that some actual distributions arise as combinations of exponential distributions by, for example, mixing or adding in the manner we considered in Chapter 2. Mixing provides a rather interesting case. In the examples considered in Chapter 2 we noted that a mixing of two distributions might be betrayed by the appearance of two humps in the histogram, although more often, mixing would not be so obvious. In the case of exponentials such obvious features of mixing cannot arise. Any exponential distribution has its largest frequency at the beginning with a steady decrease thereafter, and that feature will persist however many components there are. Nevertheless, it is interesting to know whether there is any observable property of the mixture which can be recognised by inspection of the histogram. Such a situation can be illustrated by considering a mixture of two exponentials as in Figure 3.3.

Comparing this with Figure 3.2, we notice that there are far more in the first group and the drop to the second group is much greater than for the single exponential. From that point onwards this situation is reversed, with a much reduced rate of decline. This is precisely the kind of behaviour we noticed for the distribution of the vehicle times shown in

Figure 1.6. It is thus plausible to suppose that the distribution of Figure 1.6 is actually a mixture of two exponentials. For example, it could be that the traffic flow was made up of two independent streams – private and commercial vehicles, for example. If they had been separated initially, it might be that each stream would have yielded exponential intervals. This example illustrates how such a simple method as comparing two histograms might help to formulate hypotheses for subsequent testing. This mixing hypothesis is not certain, of course, because there may be other ways in which such a distribution may have arisen – in this case there are!

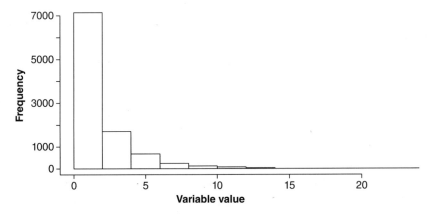

Figure 3.3 Histogram of equal mixture of two exponentials

The other way in which one pattern of variation might arise from another is by adding the variables. Therefore, we shall see what happens if we look at the distribution of the sum of two or more exponential variables. This will lead quite naturally to the third important standard distribution described in this chapter. Figures 3.4–3.6 show how the shape of the histogram changes as the number of components is increased from 2, through 10, to 100. It is clear that the form of the distribution becomes increasingly symmetrical. We have already considered partial sums of observed variables when constructing the distributions shown in Figure 2.3. Here we do it in exactly the same way, but for variables where we know the form of the distribution. As in that case, the form of the distribution becomes more symmetrical as the number of items in the sum increases. In fact the final distribution brings us very close to our third standard distribution, the Normal distribution.

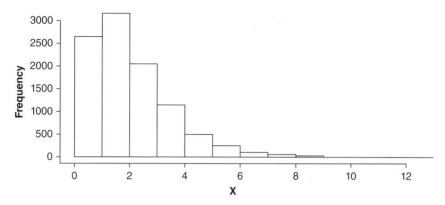

Figure 3.4 Histogram of the sum of two exponential variables

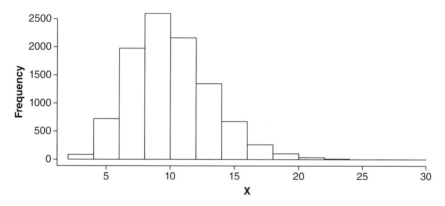

Figure 3.5 Histogram of the sum of 10 exponential variables

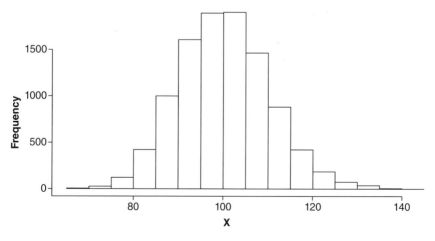

Figure 3.6 Histogram of the sum of 100 exponential variables

The Normal Distribution

The *Normal* distribution is by far the most important distribution in Statistics. Just why this is so will emerge gradually as our exposition proceeds. There is truth as well as irony in the aphorism said to be current among physical scientists that 'physicists use it because they think that mathematicians have proved its relevance and mathematicians study it because they think that physicists have found it to be an empirical fact'. There are in fact empirical and theoretical reasons for its importance, but they are so closely intertwined that it is impossible to separate them. We begin by giving an example to enable us to look at the distribution from three slightly different angles. The first two are derived from a set of 100 values of a variable which we suppose to be as follows:

> −81, 65, 58, −28, −16, 53, −132, 38, −90, 146, 48, 109, 73,
> −103, −33, 188, −36, −43, −95, −25, 39, −2, 112, −113, 29, −88,
> 147, 4, 2, −102, −13, 175, 77, 125, 39, −94, 13, 112, −190, 7, 24,
> 62, 135, −50, 121, −98, 179, 35, 54, 3, 171, −33, −45, 80, −66,
> 158, −22, 196, 49, −89, −35, −62, −42, 58, −11, 8, 178, −17, 56,
> −139, 132, 25, −36, −150, −74, 288, −64, 53, 82, 69, 26, −44, 65,
> 148, −116, 5, −152, −154, −109, 8, −17, 92, −32, 4, −109, −77, −4,
> −31, 115, 84

Notice that negative values occur; we already know that the shape of the distribution would be unaffected by shifting the whole set by adding a constant sufficient to make all values positive, but this would serve no useful purpose here.

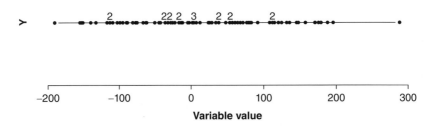

Figure 3.7 Dot diagram for Normal data

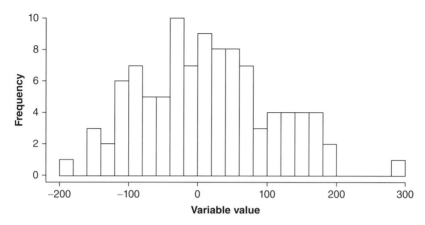

Figure 3.8 Histogram for a Normal sample

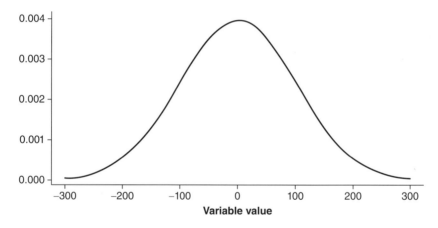

Figure 3.9 A Normal distribution

At this stage it is appropriate to ask what is meant by saying that something has a Normal, or any other, distribution. The quip 'there never was, is now and never will be a Normal distribution' contains an element of truth. For although we refer to the distribution of Figure 3.9 as a Normal distribution, it is in fact an idealisation obtained by imagining what the outline of the histogram would be if we had a very large amount of data. In practice we never have large enough amounts of data. What we actually observe is a set of data of more modest size, more like that given above and visualised in one of the ways pictured in Figures 3.7 or 3.8. Neither of the latter shows the absolute symmetry of the curve of Figure 3.9, but both are sufficiently close to the latter curve to make it credible to think of them as 'Normally distributed'. We shall be able to make this statement more precise after we have become acquainted with sampling ideas in the second half of the book. For the present the reader should have an adequate idea of what is meant by referring to a Normal distribution.

The use of the adjective 'Normal' has been disputed on the grounds that it implies that this is the sort of distribution that one 'ought' to observe. Clearly it is not, because even with the limited experience gained in the last two chapters, we know that many other diverse shapes can occur in practice. However, there is virtue in the name because the distribution does have a central place, partly for empirical reasons of which the examples considered so far give an inkling and partly because these can be given a much more secure base by a theorem in probability known as the *central limit theorem*. One alternative name for the distribution is the 'bell curve' on account of its similarity in shape to a cross-section taken through a bell.

The centrality of the Normal distribution in Statistics is mainly accounted for by the fact that adding up variables seems to induce a degree, at least, of Normality. We met an indication of this tendency in the example pictured in Figure 2.3. There we were adding up successively, 2, 4 and 8 intervals. Although the distributions of the individual components of the sums were very far from Normal, we noted the appearance of a hump which became more pronounced as the number of components in the sums became larger. We had to stop after sums of 8 components because the process had reduced the total number of intervals to a point where a reliable picture could no longer be obtained. Had we continued, it is plausible to suppose that the tendency would have become more marked. This Normalising tendency was seen much more clearly when we came to consider sums of exponential variables in Figures 3.4–3.6. Even though the constituent variable had a distribution, the exponential, far from Normal, we saw how adding them together quite rapidly produced something close to a Normal distribution. This is a truly remarkable phenomenon and is not a feature peculiar to these examples.

A second reason for the Normal distribution having a central place in Statistics arises from the fact that variables with other distributions can, sometimes at least, be transformed to a form close to Normal. We saw an example of this in Figures 2.10 and 2.11 where a logarithmic transformation of an extremely non-Normal distribution produced a Normal distribution. In one sense this is not very remarkable because any distribution can be transformed into any other – this statement must be taken on trust. What is remarkable is that such a simple transformation can produce a simple distribution by taking the logarithm. This fact offers the prospect that methods devised for Normal variables can be made more widely applicable. These remarks do not provide a totally convincing reason for the common assumption, which the reader will find in current social science research, that variability can usually be assumed to be Normal. It is not wholly clear, for example, whether the addition of variables in such contexts is present, even implicitly.

To understand how this situation has come about one needs to look back to measurement theory in the physical sciences, which has often been followed, sometimes uncritically, in the social sciences. Measurement error is important in the natural sciences, especially in physics and astronomy, where instrumentation error and human error both play a part. In fact the Normal distribution was first studied in this context where it was known simply as the *error* distribution – or the *Gaussian* distribution, after Gauss the famous mathematician. In such circumstances it was plausible to suppose that the actual error was made up of various different sources of independent error components originating in the instrument of measurement or person making the measurement. This supposition was consistent with the Normal error distributions which were observed.

Social scientists have sometimes seen an analogy here for social variability. The value of any social variable is almost certainly determined by a very large number of other variables, most of which are unknown. If one supposes that each has only a very small effect and that the total effect is roughly equal to the sum of their individual effects, the situation is analogous to that obtaining in the physical sciences. If so, it would follow that the combined effect might be approximately Normally distributed. Modest support for this argument may be obtained from the intermediate position of biometric variables. It is well attested, for example, that human height, of either males or females, is Normally distributed. Although the genetic determination of height is an extremely complex phenomenon which is not well understood, it is believed that genes play a significant part. Each relevant gene may be supposed to make only a very small contribution, but the combined effect of many genes will play a major part in determining adult height. This may account for the observed Normality of height. Taking the analogy one step further would lead us to expect that most social variables would be distributed in a form close to Normal. In practice this expectation is not always realised, but it does provide a partial justification for the common assumption. It is hardly necessary to add that assumptions of this kind should be tested empirically wherever possible.

4

SUMMARISING VARIATION

Summary

For some purposes we need to summarise a frequency distribution. Here we identify location and dispersion (or spread) as two key features and define the average (mean) and standard deviation as ways of measuring them. These measures have an important connection with the Normal distribution, which is illustrated.

Introduction

There are occasions when it is desirable to refer to particular aspects of a distribution. This will become increasingly necessary in the next chapter when we come to the decomposition of variation into parts. We have already noted how distributions can be made to differ, by shifting or by stretching, for example. In the case of the two distributions shown in Figure 2.6 there was an obvious difference, and this was described there as a shift of two units on the horizontal scale. An alternative way of specifying the difference would have been to say that the *location* had been changed by that amount. The location of a distribution summarises only one aspect of the variation; it says where on the horizontal axis the distribution is to be found. That position can be specified by a single number which summarises one particular aspect of the distribution. That number is called a *measure of location*.

Measuring Location

With a distribution like the Normal curve pictured in Figure 2.6 almost any point could have been chosen because all points move by the same amount (two units in that particular case). However, there is an advantage in using some central or typical point. The need for this is clear from Figure 2.8, where the two distributions differ in a second respect and thus not all points move by the same amount. Even so it is clear from Figure 2.8 that there is a difference in location, and this may be captured by using the central point to locate the distribution. In the case of distributions like the Normal there is little room for argument about where that central point should be. An obvious central point occurs where the curve reaches its highest point. However, in practice we do not have a smooth curve but a set of numbers, whether these are pictured by a dot diagram, as in Figure 3.7, or as a histogram, as in Figure 3.8, and it is not immediately obvious where the centre is. We shall therefore approach the question by a method which will work for the data whether specified by a histogram or a dot diagram.

First we take the continuous curve representing the frequency distribution and imagine a template of it to be cut from cardboard, plastic or some such rigid material. Next we imagine this template to be laid on a table with its base at right angles to the edge of the table. We now slide the template towards the edge of the table, making sure that the base remains at right angles to the edge. At first the template will remain flat on the table, but there will come a point where the amount overhanging will just tip the whole thing onto the floor. This will occur, as is otherwise fairly obvious, when we reach the centre line at the point where the curve reaches it maximum, dividing the template into two symmetrical halves at the point which marks the centre of the distribution. This is a good point to use as a measure of location.

This may seem an unnecessarily cumbersome way to determine the centre, but it has the advantage that it can also be used very widely and gives some insight into what we are doing. Let us continue looking at the raw data as they appear in the dot diagram of Figure 3.7. We now imagine the data as points along a rigid wire, with the data points as heavy weights. We can look for the point of balance where the data on one side will exactly balance those on the other. This point of balance marks the centre of the data in the same sense as in the experiment with the template. Readers familiar with elementary mechanics will know that this point of balance may be calculated as the average of all the values. The *average* of a set of numbers is a very familiar concept, and it is calculated by adding up the numbers and dividing by how many there are. This method will also work using a template of the histogram. The location of a distribution may thus be indicated by its average. The distributions in Figure 2.6 thus show a change in location of two units. The same may be said of the two distributions in Figure 2.8, although their location is not the only respect in which they differ.

The way in which we have arrived at the average as a measure of location will work for any distribution whatsoever, but it does not follow that the measure obtained is equally useful, or meaningful, in other contexts. In order to see whether or not this is so, we only need to note that the average of a distribution like the Normal is also associated with other properties. First, it occurs in the region of the frequency distribution where the largest frequencies occur. This might be described as the most 'populous' region. Secondly, it occurs at the point which divides the frequency into two balancing halves.

These features may be even more obvious if we compare the Normal with the exponential distribution, though much the same will also be true for any exponential-like distribution, of course. The average can be calculated for an exponential distribution, but it certainly will not occur in the most populous region which, for that distribution, is always close to zero. Neither does the average divide the distribution into parts where one part is the mirror image of the other – the values on the left of the average are all short and have a limited range while, typically, those on the right are large and very well spread out. In fact with exponential-like distributions it is hardly appropriate to use the word 'location' at all when speaking of differences between distributions since they are usually anchored to the zero point, which cannot be relocated. In fact differences between exponential-like distributions are much more sensibly thought of as differences of scale, to which we come in the next section. More generally, one might note that there is no abrupt transition from Normal-like to exponential-like distributions. As we move from one to the other the average becomes less and less suitable as a measure of location. Much will depend on whether it makes practical sense to think of the distribution as being shifted bodily in one direction or another. In practice there is no need to spend time on the details of how the average is calculated, as used to be the case in elementary courses, because this can be done now almost instantaneously using freely available computer software. The average of the data given in the previous chapter and illustrated in Figures 3.7 and 3.8 has the value 12.6, which is quite close to the centre of the distribution as displayed in those figures.

Measuring Spread (or Dispersion)

Distributions may differ in other respects. The two distributions shown in Figure 2.7 have the same location but differ in spread or dispersion. We need to pay particular attention to dispersion because our whole treatment in this book is predicated on the assumption that variation, or dispersion, is the central idea in Statistics. Figure 2.8 shows two distributions which differ in both location and dispersion. The question then naturally arises as to whether we can measure dispersion on a convenient numerical scale. Before attempting this, notice that location and dispersion differ in one other obvious respect. Location can be positive or negative because there can be a shift either to the right or the left. The dispersion, however, is necessarily positive since, by its very nature, you can only think of it as something you can have more or less of, the minimum occurring when there is no dispersion at all.

We shall demonstrate two apparently different approaches to the search for a measure of dispersion, but both lead to the same measure. The first approach builds on an idea already familiar from our work on location. If we compare two distributions which differ only in dispersion, such as those shown on Figure 2.7, it is obvious that the values of the more widely dispersed distribution tend to be farther from the average than their counterparts in the other distribution. Dispersion therefore can be said to do with distance from the average or, to use the more familiar language of measuring location, the values tend to be located farther from the average. If we work with distance from the average, therefore, we need a measure of that distance. The distance has to be measured on either side of the average. The following example shows how this is done using actual numbers:

Data	−1,	3,	4,	7,	10
Average	4.6				
Deviations from average	−5.6,	−1.6,	−0.6,	2.4,	5.4
Distances from the average	5.6,	1.6,	0.6,	2.4,	5.4

Average distance = 15.6/5 = 3.12

We have just constructed a measure which is the average distance from the average, and at a descriptive level this is a perfectly adequate measure of dispersion. Beginners in the subject encounter a puzzling feature at this point which cannot be adequately resolved at this level.

The puzzle lies in the fact that statisticians seem not to like this measure and go on to find and use another which, at first sight, appears unnecessarily complicated. Nevertheless, we shall follow them to see where the trail leads. There is more than one way of measuring distance. We may do it by taking, not the direct distance, but the square of the distance. This quantity behaves in the right way because the farther two individuals are apart, the greater will be the distance between them measured in this new way. Using the square has the advantage in that we do not have to bother about the direction in which the distance is measured, because the operation of squaring makes all distances positive. Another possible measure of dispersion, therefore, is to calculate the average of these squared distances. This average is called the *variance* and it is calculated as follows using the same data as above.

Deviations from average   −5.6,   −1.6,   −0.6,   2.4,   5.4
Squares of deviations   31.36,   2.56,   0.36,   5.76,   29.16
Variance = 69.2/5 = 13.84 (= average of squared deviations)

One further complication with the variance is that it is not measured in the same units as the original data. If, for example, the data are times expressed in minutes, the variance will be in 'minutes squared', which does not mean much to most people! This matter can be put right by using the square root of the variance which will be in the same units as the original data. This measure also has the necessary properties of a measure of dispersion and it is called the *standard deviation*. For the example given above it is 3.72. Its name, *standard deviation,* is said to have been introduced by Karl Pearson in 1894. After the average this, together with the variance, is the most important quantity in the whole of Statistics. It may help to give a glimpse, in advance, of why we have made this extravagant claim on its behalf.

Two reasons which can be given will become clearer later in this book. The first is that the standard deviation plays a very important role in relation to the Normal distribution. This is so important that we shall revisit the matter in the next section of this chapter. The second is that, if we measure dispersion using the variance, it becomes possible to split it into parts, each of which can be linked to a source of variation. It then lies at the root of the analysis of variance, which is a major part of statistical method.

There is a second way of approaching the measurement of dispersion, which is not widely known, but which leads to an equivalent measure. Knowing this may help to reduce the apparent arbitrariness of the variance. This is because the alternative measure depends only on the differences between the numbers we have observed and not on how far they are from some central measure such as the average. It may seem highly desirable on common-sense grounds to base any measure of dispersion on the differences between the values of the variable rather than on their distance from some arbitrary measure of location. However, it turns out that if we square all the differences and divide their total by the number of pairs, we get something which is just double the variance. Hence nothing extra is to be gained by going down this alternative route, however attractive it might seem. This equivalence may be illustrated for the previous example but it is true quite generally. The pairwise differences between the numbers are listed earlier and their squares are set out below:

Differences	0	−4	−5	−8	−11	Squared differences	0	16	25	64	121
	4	0	−1	−4	−7		16	0	1	16	4
	5	1	0	−3	−6		25	1	0	9	36
	8	4	3	0	−3		64	16	9	0	9
	11	7	6	3	0		121	49	36	9	0

Reading down the columns the element in the ith column and jth row is the difference between the ith and jth elements of the data. For example, −4 in the second row and 4th column is the difference between 3, the second element, and 7, which is the fourth; the square of this difference (16) is shown in the corresponding position of the right-hand table. The sum of the squared differences is 692 which, divided by 25, gives 27.68, and this is double the variance calculated above, as it should be.

Nevertheless, there is one rather trivial thing about the definition of the variance which can be very irritating. We have divided the sum of squared deviations by the number of variable values. Sometimes, for theoretical reasons, the divisor is taken as one less than this. In practice this makes hardly any difference unless we are dealing with very small numbers. The irritating thing is that the makers of pocket calculators or writers of computer software do not always make it easy to find out which definition they have used. The reader should beware.

Standard Deviation and the Normal Distribution

One reason for the importance of the Normal distribution is that it is completely known once its average and standard deviation are given, because if we know these two numbers everything about the distribution can be determined. In particular, we can find the proportion of the distribution which lies within any two values we choose to specify. In practice there are tables which tell us such things, and nowadays it is easy to find the values using a computer. We shall therefore not need to delve into such matters beyond noticing that it is useful to have a mental record of a few key features, and these are illustrated in Figure 4.1.

Here we have drawn the frequency curve for a distribution centred at zero. This is equivalent to saying that the average is zero. The important thing to notice is that the horizontal scale is marked off in multiples of the standard deviation. This means that we first have to express the values of the variable we are interested in as the appropriate multiple of the standard deviation. There is a vertical line at zero, which is the average. There are further vertical lines, symmetrically placed at distances of one and two standard deviations from the average. Virtually the whole of the distribution lies within a distance of three standard deviations from the average, and this is easy to remember. About 95% lies within a distance of two standard deviations, and because this interval will play a major role when we come to inference later, it is useful to remember this figure also. About 68%, or roughly two-thirds, of the frequency lies within one standard deviation of the average. A Normal distribution like that in Figure 4.1 is often known as the *standard Normal distribution* because it has an average at zero and a standard deviation at 1.

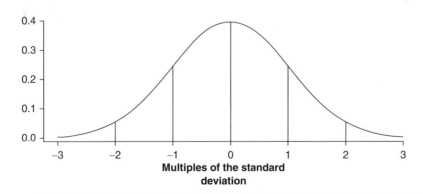

Figure 4.1 A Normal distribution with limits

If we calculate the average and standard deviation of the data used for the dot diagram of Figure 3.7 we find that the average is 12.6 and the standard deviation is 93.54. The proportion within one standard deviation is 64% and within twice the standard deviation is 98%. These are quite close to the values for the Normal distribution which were given above as 68% and 95%, respectively. Had we made the calculation for the Times(2) data used in Chapter 1 the percentages would have been less, at 78% and 94%, the latter depending on whether the value of 4 is counted as 'in' or 'out'. However, that distribution is not particularly like the Normal and the size of the data set is only 33; this suggests that our rough guides, though certainly rough, may not be that far out.

Other Summary Measures of a Distribution

For the special case of the Normal distribution there is nothing left over when the average and standard deviation have been fixed. However, this is not usually the case and it is clear why this must be so. Many distributions are not symmetrical like the Normal and when we know their averages and standard deviations there are still aspects of the distributions not specified. For example, nothing so far has been said about their asymmetry. For example, it is often useful to find a number which specifies the degree of asymmetry, called *skewness*. This can be done by extending the ideas already used in constructing the variance, but we shall not take the subject further here. Roughly speaking, virtually everything about the shape of a frequency distribution can be summed up in four numbers. These are the average and variance, which we have already met, together with measures of skewness and what is called *kurtosis*, which has to do with the degree of elongation of the tails of the distribution.

5

THE ANALYSIS OF VARIATION

Summary

The decomposition of variation is a fundamental idea in Statistics. By this means it may be possible to identify sources of variation. The problem is illustrated in this chapter using two categories, and this is then extended to many categories. Sometimes group differences conform to a linear pattern, in which case we move into regression analysis. This chapter lays the foundation for the study of many branches of statistical methodology.

Introduction

One way of exploring the reason for the patterns of variation which we observe is to investigate whether they can have arisen by lumping together variation arising from various sources. We shall thus start with a set of data and examine whether it can be decomposed into parts where each can be linked with a different source. On this account we might have used the more specific chapter title 'Decomposition of Variation' which is what we shall, in fact, be doing. However, the present title establishes an important link with a major strand in contemporary statistical analysis where the emphasis is slightly different. This chapter, in fact, deals with some of the most fundamental ideas of Statistics and, although they are the natural culmination of what has gone before, it may be best to take them slowly. In particular, especially towards the end of the chapter, the reader should expect to find it necessary to go over the ground several times.

We have already met one version of the problem we are about to tackle in the discussion of mixtures. In Chapter 2 we looked at ways in which an observed distribution could have arisen by the mixing of components, and at how we might recognise that a given distribution could have arisen in this way. Conversely, this suggested when we might look more deeply for an explanation of the shape of a distribution in terms of the components from which it was made up. Here we shall take these ideas a step further but on a more limited front.

To explain this difference of approach, let us return to an example of mixing of the kind we envisaged in Chapter 2. We now elaborate this using as an illustration an example loosely based on an actual case concerning pilot selection. Training pilots is an extremely expensive process and it is therefore desirable to identify in advance candidates who are likely to be successful. Would-be pilots may be given a simple written test to assess their suitability. The result is a score on which selection might be based. Suppose that a histogram of the scores obtained is constructed and that it has a shape somewhat like that shown in Figure 2.1. Then it would be reasonable to guess that the candidates fell into two groups, corresponding to the two peaks of the histogram. If there were some way of identifying members of these two groups in advance of the test, there might be no need to spend time and money testing those from the group having the distribution which peaked at the lower score. It is always possible, of course, that the shape of the histogram is the result of some peculiarity of the test itself – or its administration – but it would still be reasonable to explore the 'two population' theory.

The difference between the situation described above and the one which occupies this chapter, and much of the remainder of this book, is that the possibility of there being two groups in this example was, in a manner of speaking, a surprise. We were interested in the distribution of scores for all candidates and did not realise that there might be two groups present. In some situations, on the other hand, we might already have identified two possible groups and wish to know whether our prior supposition was supported by the evidence. Imagine, for example, that someone had suggested that university graduates might be better endowed for piloting than those who had been apprentices, say. In such cases we would not want to look at the combined distribution but at the individual histograms to see whether they were essentially the same, or different, in the way our hypothesis suggested. If we did find evidence of a difference we might want to go further and say something about the magnitude of that difference. We shall now investigate problems of the latter kind.

The simplest such problem concerns only two groups, but it is easy to extend the idea to several groups – or *sources* – and to the different ways in which they might be related. In essence, we shall want to know whether distributions arising from two or more groups are the same or not. At first sight this may seem a very tall order because we already know that distributions can take all sorts of shapes and the differences which might occur in comparing only two groups seem to be legion. However, things are not that bad for the following two reasons. First, in most cases the variable values whose distributions are to be compared will often be of the same kind. For example, if measures of aptitude are made on all members of two groups, it is at least plausible that they will have the same sort of distribution. Similarly, as in our next example, we shall imagine that weight loss is measured on two groups of dieters. Secondly, we can often go further by expecting the distributions to have precisely the same form, apart from where they are located. In other words, we assume that the only effect of group differences is to shift the whole distribution by an amount which depends only on the group to which they belong. We have already seen that the average is a useful measure of the location of a distribution so, for the most part, we shall be interested in whether averages differ from one group to another. It is important to remember that it is the underlying distribution which is of primary interest. This latter assumption is a strong one and arises more naturally, perhaps, in the natural sciences where the variation left over, when group differences have been accounted for, can be attributed to the error introduced by the measuring instrument. However, we have also noted that, even in the social sciences, the combined effect of all the variables unaccounted for may mimic that of a Normal distribution.

These points can be brought to a sharper focus by discussing an example of what we shall call the 'archetypal problem'. This is typical of results which are presented almost daily in the media and elsewhere.

The Archetypal Problem

Suppose the merits of two dietary regimes are being 'scientifically tested'. Two groups of dieters are selected, and one group adopts regime A and the other regime B. The questions are which of the two regimes is the better, and by how much. At this stage we shall not look into the important question of how the subjects were selected or the multitude of other matters on which the validity of the results depends.

Suppose the resulting weight losses in the two groups were as follows; the units are irrelevant to the question we are asking.

Diet A   41, 47, 27, 22, 30, 60, 51, 14, 29, 50, 48, 52, 44, 37, 35

Diet B   24, 25, 13, 7, 34, 54, 27, 31, 39, 28, 43, 55, 32, 41, 1

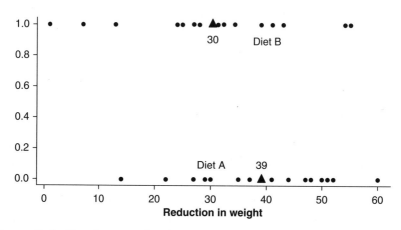

Figure 5.1 Dot diagram showing the effect of two diets

The two samples have been plotted separately in Figure 5.1, in the usual fashion, but on opposite sides of the rectangle determined by the axes. The averages are marked by solid triangles with their numerical values nearby.

Recall that the object of this exercise was to see whether the two diets were different in their effect. Following the line of development so far, we would be looking for a difference in the distributions and, in particular, a difference in their locations. There is too little data to make a judgement on the form of the distribution, but the averages tells us something about the location of the distributions and these indicate that diet A, the lower plot, has more effect than diet B, the upper plot. Is the fact that diet A has a larger average sufficient grounds for asserting that it is the better diet? I suspect that many people would be reluctant to jump to this conclusion. They might point out that there were many people on the poorer diet, as judged by this criterion, who actually lost more weight than many on the supposedly better diet. To sharpen up this judgement, imagine the losses had been tightly grouped around their respective averages. I suspect that we would then feel more confident in judging that diet A was the better. Taking this to its logical conclusion, if everyone on diet A had lost exactly 39 pounds and everyone on diet B had lost 30 pounds, I suspect there would be no difficulty in getting agreement that diet A was the better. This line of reasoning brings us close to the central question, which we shall not be able to answer fully until a later stage. Nevertheless, it seems clear from this discussion that the judgement we make should depend on the difference in the means compared with the general spread of each sample. The more dispersed the losses in the individual samples the less sure we shall be in judging one diet to be better than the other. This observation identifies the crucial fact that we must, in some way, compare the difference between the two averages with the collective differences among the individual figures. How this comparison should be made will be made clearer later in this chapter, but a complete answer must await the discussion of sampling later in the book. However, at this stage it should be quite clear that two factors must enter into the calculation: first, the difference between the averages; and secondly, the degree of dispersion in the sets of data from which those averages have been calculated. At the outset we simply asked whether the diets differed. We might have had some prior reason for expecting diet A to be better than diet B, perhaps because it involved a lower calorie intake. If so, we ought to take that prior knowledge into account also.

Before we leave this example there is another question, more periph-eral to our present interests perhaps, but whose full importance will appear later. A shrewd observer might point out that all of the people taking part in this study experienced some loss of weight. Hence, whether or not the two diets differ, one would be much more confident in asserting that dieting, on either regime, had some beneficial effect. Is this a justifiable conclusion, and what further evidence would be neces-sary for it to be fully justified? Once again, it appears that two things are relevant: first, the distance of the average for either diet from what would have happened if no one had been dieting (which over a short period should have been close to zero); and secondly, the amounts of variation in the values which have been averaged.

Comparison of Several Groups

More than two groups can be compared in much the same manner, as we shall shortly illustrate. However, there are now other possibilities opened up by the additional information provided by three or more groups. In this and the next section we shall indicate two directions in which this remark might take us.

We next imagine a situation in which we have small amounts of data giving income in six cities, which we shall call A, B, C, D, E and F.

The numbers represent amounts of money, but the units of currency are irrelevant for our purposes. They can be thought of as pounds per year, dollars per month or rupees per week, for example. This makes no difference to the points we are going to make. The data are as follows:

City A   15, 19, 16, 12, 13, 18, 11, 16, 11, 16, 8, 19, 12, 12, 11

City B   9, 13, 14, 15, 14, 12, 17, 16, 5, 11, 9, 20, 7

City C   24, 21, 12, 22, 26, 27, 25, 14, 18, 28, 19, 22, 20, 20, 14, 21, 12, 13, 18, 21, 28, 25, 14, 14, 23

City D   22, 23, 21, 20, 19, 18, 23, 30, 28, 23, 30, 23, 24, 24, 24, 35, 25, 33, 26

City E   21, 23, 15, 21, 22, 19, 19, 27, 30, 16, 23, 25, 23, 13, 25

City F   19, 29, 25, 35, 33, 25, 35, 26, 25, 21, 24

On this evidence, the initial question is: does income vary from city to city? In Figure 5.2 we look at the data in the same manner as for the last example.

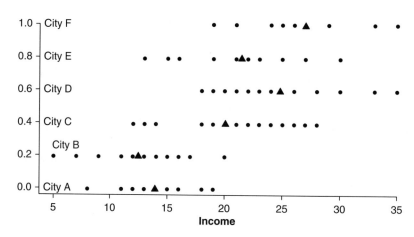

Figure 5.2 Dot diagram showing incomes in six cities

As before, the solid triangles represent the averages. In Figure 5.2 the cities are listed from bottom to top starting with city A at the bottom and ending with city F at the top. It appears from the averages that there are differences, but this variation must be judged in the light of the scatter of the solid dots, which is a matter we have deferred for later discussion.

The point of this example is to show that other questions arise once we have more than two groups. Most obvious, perhaps, is whether all cities can be separated or whether, for example, they fall into subgroups. However, we shall consider more specific patterns of difference.

Very frequently we shall know something about the cities which may help to explain any differences. Suppose, in this case, that there are two factors concerning location which may have helped to cause any differences we have observed. One factor is whether they are coastal cities, and the other is their location in a north–south direction. Each city can therefore be classified as being coastal or inland and as being north, central or south. Setting aside the variation, the average income can be calculated for each combination of the levels of these factors and the results set out in Table 5.1.

Table 5.1 Average income in cities A, ..., F classified according to location

	North	**Central**	**South**	**Total**
Coastal	24.8 (D)	21.5 (E)	27.0 (F)	24.2
Inland	13.9 (A)	12.5 (B)	20.0 (C)	16.5
All cities	20.0	17.3	22.2	

This table tells us something about the effect of location on income which was not immediately apparent from Figure 5.2. Beginning with the row totals, it is clear that income is higher in coastal cities than inland. The column totals show that there is less variation from north to south, but the central region appears to have lower income than either the north or south. The highest income of all is in southern coastal cities and the lowest in the central inland region. The variations between 'coastal' and 'inland' and between locations in a north–south direction are often called 'main effects' because they express the direct effect of location in these two aspects on income. But Table 5.1 is capable of yielding more information. In the south the differential between the coastal and inland averages is 7 units, whereas in the north the difference is 10.9. If this difference is taken at its face value, it means that the coastal versus inland effect is greater in the north than in the south. When this happens there is said to be an *interaction* between the two dimensions of location. Put a little more generally, the coastal–inland variation depends upon where the city is placed on the north–south dimension. This is precisely the same as saying that the pattern of variation is different from north to south according to whether one is on the coast or inland.

All of this raises the question of whether the factors are something we happen to identify after the event, as may appear to have been the case in this example, or whether we might exercise some choice in their selection. If this were possible the way might be open to deliberately include factors whose effect we wished to know. This is indeed possible and if pursued would take us into the realm of the design of experiments, or design of surveys.

With more groups available there is the possibility of cross-classifying them according to other factors and, if we did so, we should meet what are called *higher-order interactions*. These arise because *first-order interactions*, mentioned above, may themselves vary according to the level of some additional factor. Indeed, the position may become very complicated indeed, as may the real world which our data are intended to reveal.

The idea of interaction is one of the fundamental ideas of Statistics, and the reader should not move on until the idea has been grasped. Much confusing information is given out by the media which does not penetrate below the main effects. This is particularly the case with research on diet where, almost daily, we are told that eating more or less of something will increase life expectancy, reduce weight or achieve some other alleged desirable objective. But a diet may be more effective in some subgroups in the population than others. Very often these announcements are based only on the main effects where little is known about the interactions. The blanket statement that the result holds 'if all else is held constant' may partially cover the reputation of the investigator but does little to help the consumer. The same issue arises in many other contexts and in various guises.

Quantitative Reasons for Variation

We now consider another way in which the cities may differ. Instead of cross-classifying them according to their location, we might suspect that what really differentiated the cities was the average distance that people living in them had to travel to work. The thinking behind this might be that it would be worth travelling farther if the extra financial reward made it worth doing. The situation is now as we have displayed it in Figure 5.3. This figure differs from Figure 5.2 in two respects. The first, which is purely a matter of convention, is that income has been plotted on the vertical axis and distance on the horizontal axis. The second difference is crucial, because the spacing between the cities now reflects the varying distances of travel. The scatter of points for each time is the same as before and has the same interpretation. The completely new feature is the line running diagonally upwards, and its presence needs an explanation.

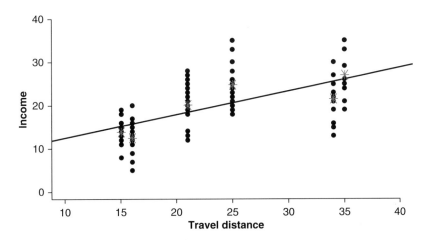

Figure 5.3 Plot of income against travel distance for six cities

Figure 5.3 represents a very simple interpretation of how income might depend on travel distance and is drawn on the assumption that income increases in proportion to travel distance. This means that an extra mile, say, would produce the same amount of extra income no matter how far the person was already travelling. If we were correct in this supposition we would expect the starred averages to lie on the line. We know that there is a good deal of variation in income for any given distance, so the relationship is far from perfect; but if the straight-line relationship held for the averages that would certainly show that there was a general tendency in the assumed direction.

Once again we must compare variations to form a judgement. The extent to which the starred points vary from the line shows us how adequate the assumption of linearity is as opposed to some other pattern of variation. The extent to which there is any relationship at all is shown by the slope of the line. To put this more directly in terms of variation, think of there being a point marked on the line where it crosses the vertical array of points. The distance from that point to the horizontal is a measure of how much work the line is doing towards explaining the relationship. As before, the vertical scatter of the black dots tells us about the variation which is still unexplained.

The Essential Idea

In this chapter the reader has met some fundamental ideas which under-lie much of statistical analysis. Because it is important to grasp at least the general idea before proceeding, we pause for a moment to repeat the essentials.

We started with the intention of decomposing variation in the hope that we could identify some of the sources of that variation. In the simplest case, we supposed that there were just two sources, and the position was illustrated in Figure 5.1. There we saw that the total variation was attributable to two sources and hence that we could think of it being made up of two parts: the variation between the two groups represented, first, by the difference between the group averages and, secondly, by the variation around those averages. There was a modest extension of the same idea in the second example. In Figure 5.2 we considered six groups whose averages differed. In addition, there was variation around each average. When considering the differences between the averages, these differences had to be judged against the inherent variation represented by their scatter around the average. At that point we had to recognise that, if we were comparing many groups, there existed the possibility of detecting more subtle patterns of variation. We showed that if the categories were the result of cross-classifying two factors, we could discover not only what are called main effects but also possible interactions between them. The final extension supposed that instead of qualitative categories the differences might be explained by a continuous variable, which in the example was distance travelled to work. In all cases the identification of effects was made by comparing the components of variation into which the original variation had been decomposed.

The Analysis of Variance

The basic idea expounded in this chapter is that we can get some idea of whether a distribution can be decomposed into one or more sub-distributions by comparing the variability of the whole data set with that of the subsets. The general idea has gained some prominence in the public discussion of the heritability of intelligence where one sometimes encounters statements of the kind 'about 50% of human intelligence is accounted for by inheritance'. We return to this topic in Chapter 13. It seems to be assumed that such statements are readily understood. Our earlier discussion has not greatly helped in this matter, since we have so far given no formal method of decomposing variance beyond arguing that it was essentially a matter of comparing the variation within components with that of the whole. In this section we shall take this argument one step further by showing how each kind of variability may sometimes be measured. We have already thought about how to measure the variability of a set of numbers, and that led to the idea of the variance. A very simple extension of this idea provides what we now need.

The argument will be illustrated using the same data which led to Figure 5.1. As a starting point, consider the first number in the first sample. This happens to be 41. We can express the distances we were looking at in the figure, arithmetically, as follows. The average for the whole data set was 34.7 and the average for the first subset was 39.1. To judge whether the two subsets were different, we would be looking at the differences 41 − 34.7 and 41 − 39.1. The first is the difference between 41 and the average of the whole set. This can be expressed as the sum of two differences as the following examples show:

distance from 41 to the subset average plus the distance from the subset average to the overall average

or, in numbers:

$$41 - 34.7 = (41 - 39.1) + (39.1 - 34.7)$$

If we were to take the second member of the second subset the corresponding decomposition would be:

$$(25 - 30.3) = (25 - 34.7) + (34.7 - 30.3)$$

If there were two distinct subsets we would expect the second difference on the right-hand side of each expression to be relatively large compared with the first. Or, what comes to the same thing, if the difference on the left-hand side were of similar magnitude to the second on the right.

This argument relates, of course, to only one particular individual in each subset. What we need is some overall collective measure embracing all such differences. This is where the idea behind the variance comes in useful. Very conveniently, it turns out that a similar relationship holds between the sums of squares of the differences. That is, for example,

$$[(41 - 34.7)^2 + (47 - 34.7)^2 + \ldots + (35 - 34.7)^2] + [(24 - 34.7)^2 + \ldots + (1 - 34.7)^2]$$

$$= [(41 - 39.1)^2 + (47 - 39.1)^2 + \ldots + (35 - 39.1)^2]$$

$$+ [(24 - 34.7)^2 + (25 - 34.7)^2 + \ldots + (1 - 34.7)^2]$$

$$+ 15[(39.1 - 34.7)^2 + (30.3 - 34.7)^2]$$

The 15 in the last line is the size of each subset. The first line of this expression is called the *total sum of squares* (TSS) because it is the sum of the squared differences of all the data set from the average of the whole set. The second and third lines are known as the *within-groups sum of squares* (WGSS), and there we take the differences from the subset averages rather than from the overall average. The last line is the *between-groups sum of squares* (BGSS), which depends on the difference between the group averages. In brief,

TSS = WGSS + BGSS

If the BGSS comprises the larger part of the TSS, this suggests that the separation of the two subsets is important. For the foregoing example TSS = 6222.3, WGSS = 5632.7 and BGSS = 589.6, which adds up as it should. Most of the variation is thus within the subsets. In practice, of course, it is not necessary to make the calculations in this fashion because this is taken care of by appropriate software. The details are spelt out here to give some insight into what is involved in making the comparison.

A similar analysis may be carried out on the extended data set used for Figure 5.2. Here there is the slight complication that there are unequal numbers in the subsets, but, taking this into account, the decomposition of the total sum of squares turns out to be as follows:

TSS = 4253.9,　BGSS = 2297.9,　WGSS = 1956.0

Here the BGSS constitutes a larger proportion of the TSS than in the two-subset example.

You might wonder whether we can obtain an overall picture of the variation arising from different sources in the case of the two extensions which lay behind Table 5.1 and Figure 5.3. The answer is 'yes' in the case of the effect of distance travelled, and we take that first, although we shall not pursue the matter in detail.

When we looked at the effect of distance travelled to work we noticed that the variation could be decomposed into several parts. One part could be explained by supposing that there was an underlying straight-line relationship between distance travelled and income. This left rather a lot of variation unexplained, but part of what was left over could be attributed to departure from the line and the rest remained unexplained. It is possible to do much the same for the overall picture by calculating sums of squares whose values summarise each of those components. The resulting partition may be described as an *analysis of variance*.

When we come to the other example where the variation in income between locations was cross-classified, the position is a little more complicated. In that case people were classified according to which combination of the factors applied in their case. Had the numbers in these categories been equal, we could have separated out the effects of location and constructed sums of squares reflecting the effect of the coastal–inland variation and that of north–south variation. But these numbers were not equal so, at the present level of our treatment, we are unable to do this. However, it was still useful to look at the variation in the manner illustrated.

6

COVARIATION

Summary

We now move on to the study of relationships between variables. This is done first from a correlation and then from a regression perspective. We define the correlation coefficient and emphasise the point that correlation does not imply causation. Then we consider the prediction of one variable given another variable and introduce the principle of least squares.

Introduction

Covariation is about how the variation of one variable depends upon that of another. It may, of course, depend on several other variables also, but our main focus in this chapter will be on the case when there is only one such variable. Such problems are known as *bivariate* problems. If more variables are involved we have a *multivariate* problem.

We have already met one bivariate problem where, in the previous chapter, we were interested in how income depended on distance travelled to work. In particular, we were interested in whether distance could explain some of the variation in income. Here we shall be able to set that particular problem in a wider context. Bivariate data often occur in social science research. If we conduct a survey, we will normally obtain a number of pieces of information on each subject and a bivariate analysis will enable us to look at them in pairs. For example, we might obtain the number of people in the household and the number of rooms occupied, or data on voting intentions and hobbies.

Broadly speaking, bivariate problems fall into two categories. First, there are those concerned primarily with prediction, or explanation, like the example mentioned above. Secondly, there are those where the two variables are on an equal footing and we want to describe, or measure, the strength of the relationship between them. This is not a rigid distinction and sometimes we shall move, almost imperceptibly, from one to the other.

We shall begin, as we did in Chapter 1, with some data on sentence length. The difference here is that we shall look at two measures of length instead of one. In order to illustrate the range of possibilities we shall use two examples. The first shows the relationship between the number of words and number of letters. The number of words in a sentence is not the only way of measuring sentence length; the number of letters is another, as, less directly, is the number of vowels. This immediately raises the question of whether there is a 'best' way and what might be lost if we used one variable rather than the other. This focuses our attention on the relationship between measures, and here we look first at the relationship of sentence length measured by words or letters. The letter lengths for what we called the Times(1) passage were as follows:

155, 87, 179, 76, 100, 224, 78, 75, 22, 104, 108, 37, 186, 186, 57, 150, 161, 77, 76, 151, 152, 85, 117, 44, 120, 146, 182

The lengths, as measured by words, have been seen before in Chapter 1 and will be used again here; the numbers of letters are new. Each variable can, of course, be looked at individually by the methods of that chapter, but here we concentrate on the relationship between them.

The first way of introducing some order, which we have used before, is to arrange the numbers in increasing order of magnitude. Here little would be gained by doing that, because in doing it for one set we should destroy it for the other; unless, of course, both series happen to have the same rank order. The second thing was to construct a dot diagram as in Figure 1.1. We can do this for the bivariate data by using a two-dimensional plot, where one variable is plotted against the horizontal axis and one against the vertical axis. This has been done in Figure 6.1.

For the second example we have paired the lengths of words in the Times(1) article with those in Times(2), in the order in which they occurred in the original passages. That is, we pair the first sentence length in the Times(1) passage with the first in the Times(2) passage, the second in the one with the second in the other, and so on. The first two pairs are thus (27, 9) and (23, 11). This is a somewhat artificial procedure but it will serve for illustration. The resulting dot diagram is given in Figure 6.2. Comparing Figures 6.1 and 6.2, we notice a radical difference on which we shall comment later.

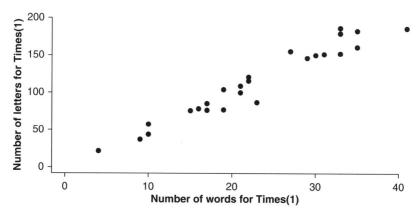

Figure 6.1 Number of letters per sentence plotted against number of words per sentence for the Times(1) data

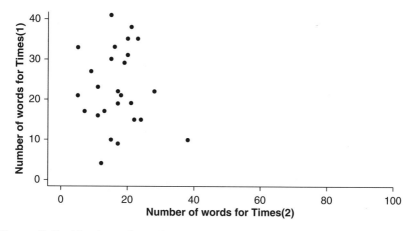

Figure 6.2 Number of words per sentence for Times(1) plotted against number of words per sentence for Times(2)

The next step we took in looking at variability with a single variable was to construct a frequency distribution by recording how many values fell into suitably chosen categories. This was central to all our subsequent work because it provided a summary of the variation which, we have claimed, is central to the understanding of statistical ideas.

TABLE 13 (Special Data)

RELATIVE NUMBER OF BROTHERS OF VARIOUS HEIGHTS TO MEN OF VARIOUS HEIGHTS, FAMILIES OF FIVE BROTHERS AND UPWARD BEING EXCLUDED

Heights of the men in inches	Heights of their brothers in inches													Total cases	Medians
	Below 63	63.5	64.5	65.5	66.5	67.5	68.5	69.5	70.5	71.5	72.5	73.5	Above 74		
74 and above	1	1	...	...	...	...	...		1	...	5	3	12	24	
73.5	...	...	...	...	...	1	3	4	8	3	3	2	3	27	
72.5	...	...	...	...	1	1	6	5	9	9	8	3	5	47	71.1
71.5	...	1	...	1	2	8	11	18	14	20	9	4	...	88	70.2
70.5	...	...	1	1	7	19	30	45	36	14	9	8	1	171	69.6
69.5	...	1	2	1	11	20	36	55	44	17	5	4	2	198	69.5
68.5	...	1	5	9	18	38	46	36	30	11	6	3	...	203	68.7
67.5	2	4	8	26	35	38	38	20	18	8	1	1	...	199	67.7
66.5	4	3	10	33	28	35	20	12	7	2	1	...	...	155	67.0
65.5	3	3	15	18	33	36	8	2	1	1	...	...	...	110	66.5
64.5	3	8	12	15	10	8	5	2	1	...	...	...	...	64	65.6
63.5	5	2	8	3	3	4	1	1	...	1	...	...	1	20	
Below 63	5	5	3	3	4	2	...	...	...	...	...	...	1	23	
Totals	23	29	64	110	152	200	204	201	169	86	47	28	25	1329	

Figure 6.3 Table extracted from Galton's *Natural Inheritance*

The pictorial representation of that frequency distribution was a histogram. In the case of two variables we would have to record how many values fall into categories formed by the suitable division of both variables. In the case of sentence and word length we have deliberately used only small sets of data to keep the mechanics of handling it as transparent as possible, but this is not a sufficient number to make the present point effectively. To carry the story further we need a larger set, and for this we shall use a bivariate distribution of great historical interest, obtained by Sir Francis Galton towards the end of the nineteenth century. Galton was interested in inheritance, and his book *Natural Inheritance* was published in 1898. It contains much other data relating to the inheritance of various physical characteristics, and he attempts to draw out their implications. Some of the most interesting examples relate to human height as it varies between and within generations. The data relating to inheritance of height from fathers to sons are, perhaps, the most famous and have been used as an ingredient of many elementary Statistics courses, as a cursory search of the Web will show. Here we shall use his data on the relationship between male heights within the same family and generation. Characteristically, Galton gives a very thorough account, in the text of the chapter, of the origin of the data as it bears on their interpretation, but we shall omit this because our interest is solely in what a bivariate distribution looks like and what its components mean. Galton's original Table 13 on page 210 of his book is reproduced here as Figure 6.3. The last column can be ignored for our purposes.

Because height varies continuously, values have been grouped into intervals of 1 inch and the mid-points of the intervals are given in the row and column labels. There were 1329 pairs of brothers, and this total number appears at the bottom right of the table. We may think of the range of height as divided into 'cells' defined as the regions bounded by the row and column intervals. The cell frequencies are recorded in the body of the table. Thus, for example, there were 14 pairs where a man had height in the interval 71–72 inches and his brother was in the interval 70–72 inches.

The final column and the last row of the table, headed 'Total cases' and 'Totals', give what are called the *marginal* distributions. These are frequency distributions of exactly the same kind as those we met in Chapter 1 and they tell us how height varies in the male populations. In this particular case both marginal distributions should be much the same, because of the arbitrariness of which member of a pair is designated as the 'man' and which the 'brother'. In fact this does seem to be the case, but it is of no immediate interest here. With any bivariate distribution we may, in addition, want to look at either margin as of interest in its own right.

The new feature is provided by the other rows and columns of the table. If we look, for example, at the row for men with height between 70 and 71 inches, we have the frequency distribution of brother's height for men within that interval. This is an example of a *conditional* distribution. This tells us how 'brother's height' is distributed for men with that particular height. The concept of a conditional distribution is the fundamental idea when dealing with bivariate or multivariate data. When there is more than one variable, the marginal distribution is not sufficient; we have to look at the conditional distributions also because it is they that tell us about how the distribution of one variable depends on the values of other variables. In particular, we may be interested in how the average of one variable depends on known values of the other, or others. In effect this is what we were doing in the previous chapter where we were interested in how income depended on distance travelled to work.

Measurement of Covariance and Correlation

Although our main emphasis has been on using the whole frequency distribution as a means of understanding variability, it is sometimes useful to summarise such distributions by a single measure which encapsulates some key feature. This was the case with the average and the variance. Now we seek to do the same sort of thing with measuring relationships. We start with what is called the covariance which, under certain circumstances, becomes the correlation coefficient. The need for such a measure becomes apparent if we imagine having several tables like that in Figure 6.3. Each might show some degree of correlation, but we might want to go further and say which showed the strongest relationship, which the second and so on. More generally, it turns out that many advanced techniques much used by social scientists make measures of covariance their starting point.

When constructing a measure of dispersion we noted that the difference between an observation and its average was the key thing. If we measured this by the square of this difference the average of these quantities became our measure of variation. With bivariate data, observations come in pairs. Our method will be first to consider a single pair from which we will devise a measure of how much it might contribute to the covariance; the covariance will then be formed from the magnitude of these contributions. Let us consider one such pair and look at the distance of each from their respective averages.

The first member of the Times(1) data set was 27 and the average of the whole data set was 23.1. The first member of the Times(2) data set was 9 and the average was 16.3. The deviation in the first case is +2.9 and in the second case is −7.3. If the two lengths had had the same sign and both were a similar distance from their respective averages, that would have been suggestive of large values of one being associated with large values of the other. In this case this is not so; they have opposite signs and the product of the distance is therefore negative. Taking the data as a whole, a preponderance of positive products will be indicative of a positive relationship, whereas a preponderance of negative products will suggest the opposite. The average of these products will thus indicate in which direction any association lies. This is not the only way of combining the products to achieve this end, but it is certainly one of the simplest. The average of these contributions is called the *covariance*. In support of this way of doing the calculation we might notice that, if the two variables are identical, the method would yield the variance.

The trouble with the covariance as we have defined it is that it depends on the scale of measurement, whereas for many purposes it is more appropriate to use a measure which does not depend on scale in this way. Had we multiplied the sentence lengths by 10, for example, the covariance would have been multiplied by 100. Independence of scale can easily be achieved by measuring our original variables in units of their standard deviation. Each value then tells us how far it is from its average in units of the standard deviation. A covariance measured in this way is called the *correlation coefficient*. A value of 0 is indicative of no correlation at all, and it can vary between −1 and +1, either extreme denoting a perfect relationship in a positive or negative direction. In the case of Figure 6.1 the correlation coefficient is 0.97 and in the case of Figure 6.2 it is −0.08. The former value is very close to 1, indicating a very strong relationship, and the latter value is close to zero. These two numbers confirm what we might have expected from the figures. The number of words in a sentence is something which must be roughly proportional to the number of letters, unless the author is making a special effort to use shorter words in long sentences or vice versa. This seems extremely unlikely! When making the comparison of sentence lengths in the two articles, Times(1) and Times(2), there is no reason to expect any relationship at all between the writing of two different authors or even the same author, and this is confirmed by the very small value of the correlation coefficient.

The interpretation of correlation is beset by hazards. The whole problem can be summed up in the mantra: *correlation does not imply causation*. A correlation merely tells us whether two variables increase, or decrease, together. The value obtained says nothing about causation, yet the temptation to make this link is such that the two are often confused. Correlations which do not indicate causation are sometimes called nonsense, or better still, *spurious* correlations. One of the least subtle forms of the error arises when events are occurring in time. Most variables increase, or decrease, as time passes and thus inevitably will be correlated whether or not there is any causal link between them. For example, if the weekly unemployment figures are rising in spring and if sea temperatures are also on the rise, no one is likely to suggest, because of that, that the two variables are directly connected. However, the error is often not so blatant and is often passed off by the media as scientific fact. For example, it was reported that individuals who ate seven portions of fruit and vegetables a day seemed to be healthier than those who had the recommended five a day. This may not be all it seems, because the better off might be able to afford more of these things, as well as other products conducive to good health. A better-established, though somewhat well-worn, example concerns the relationship between smoking and lung cancer. It has been known for a long time that exposure to tobacco smoke and lung cancer are correlated. However, it was pointed out that this correlation need not mean that tobacco smoke was the cause of lung cancer. It could be, for example, that a third factor such as the pollution by exhaust fumes was the real cause, because smokers were more likely to live in urban environments where atmospheric pollution was greater. In other words, a third factor, living in an urban environment, was associated both with smoking and cancer. Another, more recent, example is provided by the alleged dependence of the risk of heart disease on the consumption of saturated fat. This problem is complicated by the fact that there are several kinds of unsaturated fat, meaning that reduction in consumption of one kind of food may be accompanied by changes in the consumption of others and also that the general level of intake of calories may have changed.

It is very rare for it to be useful to quote a single correlation coefficient by itself, since there are almost always other variables involved, whose effects will impinge on the apparent relationship between any pair of variables. Nevertheless, the correlation coefficient is a fundamental quantity in much multivariate analysis, and the reader who moves on to more advanced work will meet it again there. In Chapter 13 we shall give a glimpse of some of the possibilities. These build on the rather curious fact that the notion of spurious correlation can, in fact, be turned to advantage. For the mutual correlation of several variables can sometimes be a sign that there is a further unobserved but important variable, which is responsible for what, taken by itself, might be interpreted as spurious.

Principle of Least Squares

Here we shall introduce an important method of Statistics in the context of what is perhaps the simplest of all applications of the idea. The problem is to fit a straight line to a bivariate scatter plot as shown in Figure 6.1. The linear relationship is suggested by the plot itself, but also because we would expect just such a relationship from the way in which sentences are constructed. There are many practical contexts where similar problems arise, and it is therefore useful to know how to 'fit' a line to the data. It may not be immediately obvious what fitting a line has to do with measuring the relationship between the two variables, which we have just been discussing. The two problems are, in fact, very closely related. In technical terms this relationship exists because covariance measures the strength of linear relationship.

One obvious way to fit a line is to draw one by eye, which in this case is quite easy because the points are so tightly located around the line. In general, however, the scatter is greater and there would be more room for argument about which line was best. What is needed is some objective method of selecting what might be called the 'best' line on which everyone might agree. Such a method is provided by the *principle of least squares*.

First we need some method of measuring how good any proposed line is, and we can then move it around until the measure of closeness is as small as possible. Imagine a line superimposed on Figure 6.1. If we want a line for predicting the number of words, we could measure the error of each prediction for each of the points where we have evidence. If there are 27 points, as in this example, we shall have 27 'errors', each error being the distance from the actual number of words to the values predicted by the line. Ideally these should all be zero, but we shall find that, as we move the line to reduce some distances, others will be increased. We thus have to decide where to make a compromise. According to the principle of least squares, we measure the overall fit of the line by squaring each difference and adding up the squares. Using the squares should come as no surprise after meeting a similar problem with the variance.

There are mathematical ways of doing this with which we are not concerned here. The important thing is to understand what it is we are trying to do. Figure 6.4 shows the line fitted by the principle of least squares superimposed on Figure 6.1.

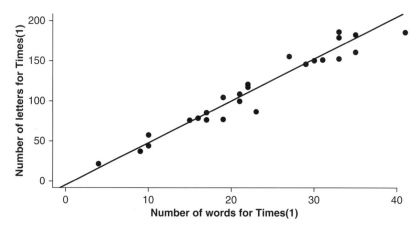

Figure 6.4   Line fitted by least squares to predict number of letters from number of words, Times(1)

The vertical distances from each point to the line are the errors of prediction we would make if we were to use the line to predict the number of letters for each sentence length in our data. It is the sum of the squares of these distances that we have minimised when finding the line. The purpose behind fitting the line, of course, would be to have a handy tool for predicting the number of letters for any number of words over the range covered.

Arbitrarily, we have supposed that the number of words is given and that we wish to predict the number of letters. But suppose we had wanted to do things the other way round; could we use the same line? Obviously we could, but we can do better by fitting another line specifically for making that type of prediction. This is easily done by interchanging the roles of the two variables and looking at the horizontal instead of the vertical distances. If we do this and superimpose the new line on the old one on Figure 6.4 we obtain the result shown on Figure 6.5.

The two lines are very close, because the points lie quite close to a line, but they are not identical. There is no reason why they should be, because it is the horizontal distances which we are looking at in the second case. Had there been a much looser scatter the difference between the two lines would have been greater.

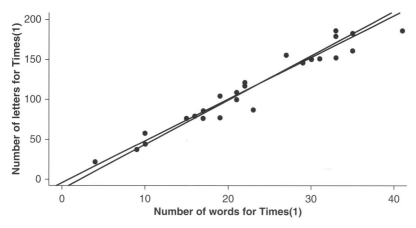

Figure 6.5 Lines fitted by least squares to predict number of letters from number of words and vice versa

The two lines we have fitted are known as *regression* lines. The term 'regression' is used for historical reasons and has no particular meaning in most applications. It goes back to Francis Galton who used the method in studying the relationship between the heights of fathers and sons and spoke of 'regression to the mean' to describe the fact that, although tall fathers tended to have tall sons, the sons, though tall, would tend to have a height somewhat closer to the average than their father.

There is nothing special about fitting a straight line, and we can fit any other curve in the same manner. We would not want to do that in the present case because the data, and what we know about the structure of language, strongly suggest that any relationship must be linear. In general, however, the same idea will work whatever shape of curve we want to fit. As before, we measure the vertical distances between the points and the proposed curve and add up their squares. This sum of squares measures how good that particular curve is. The position of the curve is then adjusted so as to make this measure as small as possible.

The principle of least squares is an example of a general method used very widely in Statistics. The line is an example of a statistical *model*. That is to say, it is a theoretical description of how the two variables might be related – not in this example only, but possibly in many other situations where the same two variables might be encountered. The general method, which we described, is to devise some measure of how closely a particular instance of the model fits the data and then to continue adjusting the model until the fit is as close as possible.

7

SAMPLING

Summary

This chapter marks a change of viewpoint from description to inference. Chapters 1–6 are concerned with variation as it actually occurs; Chapters 7–13 look at the consequences of sampling variation. This chapter lays the groundwork by discussing the process of sampling itself. The focus is on simple random sampling, but other kinds of sampling are briefly mentioned.

Introduction

This chapter marks a turning point in our development of statistical ideas without mathematics. Thus far we have looked at collections of data and concentrated on describing the variability which they exhibited. That was a legitimate end in itself, but we have not asked much about where the data came from or whether the conclusions drawn from them had a wider applicability. For example, we looked at time intervals between passing vehicles on a road. These were observed at a particular place on a particular day, and we might have wondered whether similar results might have been obtained on another day at another place. In other words, we might have been interested in whether or not our conclusions could be generalised. In this and the following chapters we shall focus on what can be inferred from the sample in hand to the wider world of which it is a part.

There are many important situations where we are not dealing with samples. National censuses, for example, aim to cover the whole population, and, so far as they are relevant, the methods of the foregoing chapters provide all that is required. Frequently, however, it is not possible to observe the whole population, and we then want to infer as much as possible from a sample. Much of statistical methodology aims to provide tools for this job.

Before going farther it will be useful to define more precisely two of the terms which we have already used in an imprecise and everyday sense. A *population* is the collection of things about which we wish to make inferences. A *sample* is a part of a population which has been obtained for the purpose of making such inferences. The term 'population' makes one think of human populations and, initially at least, it is useful to speak in those terms. However, the term is used much more widely to embrace any collection of items. For example, we might be interested in all the words in a book or newspaper, all the fish in a lake, all the intervals between passing vehicles at specified sites in a week, month or year and so on. There are even cases where the population may be effectively infinite, but that poses conceptual problems which we shall bypass for the moment. This chapter is about obtaining samples; the following chapters move on to the problem of how to draw inferences from those samples.

Intuition suggests that, if a sample is to be useful, it should be representative of the population, but therein lies a paradox. If we could know that a sample was representative – meaning that it was a kind of population in miniature – we would obviously know something about the population itself. But finding out something about the population is the whole point of drawing a sample in the first place! Obviously we need some method of drawing samples which can be trusted to give a good likeness of the population, most of the time at least. This statement immediately draws attention to a very important qualification which applies to any adjective which we attach to the word 'sample'. It must refer to the method by which the sample was obtained and not to the character of the sample itself. We cannot tell by simply looking at a sample whether it will allow legitimate inferences. We need to know how it was obtained. In feeling our way to a satisfactory method of drawing samples it is convenient to approach the subject negatively because it appears much easier to identify unsuitable than suitable methods. Continuing to think in terms of human populations, we would avoid methods which involve interviewing people in the street because this would disproportionately omit those who were housebound. Similarly, interviews by telephone during working hours would bias the sample in favour of those who were not housebound. The word *bias* highlights what it is we wish to avoid. A sample is biased if it is disproportionately weighted towards any particular subgroup whose responses might be atypical. We only say 'might' because there is no knowing whether being housebound, for example, is in any way related to the subject of enquiry. The important thing is to exclude any possible source of bias. The only way to do this is to ensure that no member of the population has an advantage in the process of selection. Or, to put it another and more exact way, to achieve this by making sure that every possible sample has the same chance of being selected. This method is known as *simple random sampling*. It is not the only valid method of sampling, but the idea lies at the root of all such methods. To make sure that this is clear we shall illustrate the position by a simple example. The example is absurdly simple, because no one in their right mind would ever need to sample from such a small population, but it serves to exemplify the principle involved on a scale which is readily grasped.

Suppose that we have a population of six members made up of the first six sentences of the Times(1) data set given in Chapter 1. To distinguish one sentence from another we give the sentences the labels A, B, C, D, E, F. The population is therefore

```
A    B    C    D    E    F
27   23   33   15   21   38
```

The possible samples of size 3 are:

ABC ABD ABE ABF

ACD ACE ACF

ADE ADF

AEF

BCD BCE BCF

BDE BDF

BEF

CDE CDF

CEF

DEF

There are thus 20 possible samples of size 3. Under simple random sampling each of these must have the same chance of selection. Note that A occurs in 10 samples, as does each of the other population members;

each therefore has the same chance of being selected. In practice, of course, the population size would be much larger and the number of possible samples very large indeed. However, we are here concerned with principles and not with the mechanics of drawing samples in practice, to which we shall come later. Not all of the samples listed above would be described as 'representative' in the ordinary sense of the word. For example, the sample BDE consists of the smallest word lengths, and if this was all we observed we might be misled into thinking that sentence lengths are smaller than they actually are. Against this it might be argued that that particular sample was unlikely to be drawn. With examples like this we get a glimpse of some of the inevitable consequences of simple random sampling. We might hope that, with very much larger populations and somewhat larger sample sizes, the chance of getting wildly untypical samples would be negligible.

There is another way of sampling which is equivalent to the one we have just described. This lends itself more readily to a practical way of sampling, but we think the definition already given, which gives all samples an equal chance of selection, is the more appealing intuitively. The method is as follows. We draw the first member of the sample in such a way that every member of the population has the same chance of selection. The second member is drawn in the same way from those that remain. The third member is drawn from those that remain after the second drawing, and so on in the same fashion until the required sample size has been achieved. This is sometimes described as *sampling without replacement* and is the method which is almost always used.

Drawing a Simple Random Sample

It is clear that it would be extremely tedious to list all possible samples, and to devise a method of selecting one of them at random. Conceptually, we might think of each sample's name being written on a slip of paper or a ball and of one ball being drawn after they have been thoroughly 'mixed up'. A lottery provides a more practical example of how a random sample might be drawn. There the aim might be to draw a winning set of numbers from a very large population of possible combinations. In lotteries the method has to be both theoretically credible and visually impressive. In survey sampling, things are rather more straightforward – in principle at least.

The first, and crucial step, is to reduce all sampling problems to a standard form. This is done by linking each population member to a number and then drawing a sample from the population of numbers.

The process is further facilitated by the availability of tables, or latterly computer programs, which provide ready-made samples. The key to justifying and understanding this process is the idea of random numbers – which we have already met in Chapter 3. In practice, then, it is only necessary to specify the sizes of the population and the sample and the computer will provide the numbers of the population which are to be included in the sample.

The procedure we have described may be seen as a counsel of perfection. It is sometimes possible to use it exactly as described, but there are many practical difficulties, some of which we cover below, standing in the way of implementation. Nevertheless, it is important to be clear about the ideal for which we are aiming, because the theory upon which inference from the sample to the population relies assumes random sampling.

It is worth mentioning *quota sampling* in this context. It is very widely used, especially by commercial organisations, because it is relatively cheap and easy to carry out. It is not a valid method of random sampling and it would be out of place to provide an adequate rationale here. It is mentioned only because it happens to be related to stratified sampling to which we come shortly. It differs from stratified random sampling only at the final, but crucial, stage. Instead of selecting from the chosen strata at random, the selection is made by interviewers in a manner which they judge to be representative of the stratum members. It therefore gains all the benefits of stratified random sampling which stem from the stratification itself. It loses by introducing a subjective element in place of random sampling at the final stage. If there is a complex system of stratification, the benefits may be considerable and worth the risk of what is sacrificed at the final stage.

Other Random Sampling Methods

A simple random sample can be drawn without knowing anything at all about the population members except for some identifying characteristic. In the case of human populations this may be a name or address. In practice we often have more information about sample members, and as this may be relevant to the object of the enquiry, it would be a pity not to make use of it. For example, we may know the age, place of residence or occupation of population members. It would seem sensible to make sure that our sample reflects the composition of the population in these respects. We do not know in advance, of course, whether the subject of our enquiry is correlated with any of these known factors, but by including them in the design we make sure that they are not overlooked.

This is done by what is called *stratified random sampling*. The sub-populations formed according to place of residence, or whatever, are called *strata*. This makes it possible to sample separately from each stratum. It also offers the prospect of sampling some strata more intensively if that offers the benefit of greater precision. For example, if the strata had been formed on the basis of educational level reached, it might be that incomes varied relatively little within some strata and there might therefore be an advantage in sampling relatively fewer individuals from those strata. Texts on sample design for finite populations go into these matters in much more detail.

Sampling finite populations of humans may be very expensive, and there are designs which are intended to minimise costs. The location of potential respondents will involve interviewer travelling costs in face-to-face surveys. Having arrived at a remote location, for example, it may pay to obtain more information from respondents near that location because that involves very little additional travelling and so is relatively cheap. *Cluster sampling* is designed to take advantage of this possibility. The term *cluster* expresses the idea that the population is grouped around particular locations. The simplest cluster sampling design involves two stages: first we select clusters, and then the individuals within a cluster. This is done in such a manner as to minimise the total cost of sampling – or to get the optimum allocation within a given budget.

Without wishing to digress into the practical hazards of using samples from finite populations, it is important to remember that, even though we have used a random sampling technique, the sample available for analysis may have a number of biases. Respondents who are unobtainable, or refuse to respond, for example, may well not be typical and so their absence biases the whole sample.

Drawing Samples from a Distribution

What we have just described is sometimes known as 'sampling from finite populations', but many collections of data do not fit into this framework. If, for example, we are measuring response times in a psychological experiment, there may be no well-defined population of subjects and the times yielded by any one subject may just be a single value. If the experiment were to be repeated, different times would be obtained by the same subject and these might well be affected by fatigue, and so, in effect, are not sampled from the same population. In what sense, then, are the values in such an experiment a random sample, and if they are, what is the population?

Progress can only be made by assuming that the data obtained may be treated *as if* they had been obtained by random sampling from *some* population. This is sometimes described as 'sampling from an infinite population', but it would be more accurate to speak of a population of 'indefinite' size. In practice the set of data is treated *as if* it was a simple random sample from a large population of such measurements in which the values had a particular frequency distribution. The question then is: how do we obtain a random sample from a population in which we know that the variable in which we are interested has a specified distribution? There is no limit on the number of such observations we could make, and so there is no very satisfactory definition of the population itself. There is no question, therefore, of identifying each population member with a number and then drawing samples using a table of random numbers. We could imagine a very large collection of data having a histogram conforming to the specified distribution and then treat that as a finite population from which we could sample in the manner described above. What we actually do is, in fact, very close to that. Again, we start with a set of random numbers from a table or generated by a computer. As we saw in Chapter 3, these numbers may be regarded as a sample from a rectangular distribution. The link lies in the fact that any distribution can be transformed into any other distribution by an appropriate transformation – shifting, stretching and squeezing, as we called it in Chapter 2. Given that a random number generator provides random samples from a uniform distribution, we can therefore transform them into random samples from any other distribution we choose. This is the method we used for producing the data we used in Chapter 3 to illustrate the shapes of the exponential distributions and Normal distributions pictured in Figures 3.2 and 3.8.

Transformation is not the only way to generate samples with a distribution of known form. Adding variables is another such method, and in Chapter 9 we shall meet further examples. Indeed, one of the most important and remarkable results in Statistics, expressed in what is known as the *central limit theorem*, says that Normal distributions can often be obtained, approximately, by simply adding up variables having almost any other distribution.

8

INTRODUCTION TO THE IDEAS OF INFERENCE

Summary

The key idea underlying this chapter is the sampling distribution. This chapter outlines some of the basic ideas of hypothesis testing and confidence intervals and introduces some terminology, including significance and P-value.

Introduction

Statistical inference concerns drawing conclusions about a population on the evidence of a sample taken from it. The possibility of doing this depends upon how the sample has been obtained. In the previous chapter we faced the problem of how to choose a sample which was representative, and concluded that a simple random sample was the simplest way of doing this. It is the method of drawing the sample which provides the bridge from the data that we have, the sample, to the data we would like to have had, the population. Such sampling methods are sometimes described as *probability sampling* because of the implicit probabilistic element in the definition in the sampling method. We have deliberately played down this aspect because probability ideas have not been used so far, although the notion underlies the more intuitive idea of all samples being 'equally likely'.

Inference is often seen as one of the more difficult aspects of Statistics, but it plays a dominant role in many presentations of the subject, including many at the elementary level. We shall therefore approach it in easy stages, contending that most of the ideas are familiar in everyday reasoning. The only difference here is that they are refined and made more precise. A central idea is that of the sampling distribution, but we have deferred this to the next chapter because it is possible to lay the foundation before bringing that concept into the picture.

The Essence of the Testing Problem

We begin by posing a very simple question, the answer to which introduces the essential ideas without introducing any new concepts. Could a given observation have come from some specified distribution? Although such a question rarely arises in practice in this form, it may be regarded as the prototype of virtually all hypothesis testing problems. It is therefore worth analysing it in some detail. We have already used the word 'hypothesis' and shall continue to use it to refer to any proposition about a frequency distribution that we wish to put to the test, although a formal definition must wait until Chapter 9. The precise way in which we go about answering this question depends to some extent on the form of the distribution which is being tested. To avoid such complications we shall first suppose the distribution under test is Normal, or at least shares the 'Normal' characteristic of tailing off towards either extreme. The position we face is expressed in Figure 8.1. Although the distribution shown has a standard deviation of 1 it can, of course, represent any Normal distribution if the horizontal scale is taken to be in units of the standard deviation.

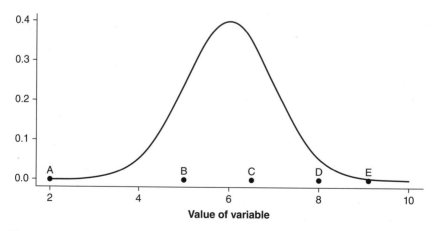

Figure 8.1 Possible values of a variable to be judged against a Normal distribution with average 6 and standard deviation 1

Five possible variable values are shown on the figure, identified by the letters, A, ..., E, and we shall consider the hypothesis that each, in turn, has been drawn randomly from the Normal distribution which is also shown. Let us begin with B and C. Both are in the region where values frequently occur with this distribution, so their occurrence would occasion no surprise. Neither gives us any grounds for supposing that they were not drawn at random from this Normal distribution. It is very important to notice that this is not the same as saying that they are very likely to have come from this distribution. It is obvious that they could equally well have come from any other distribution centred in the same area. The correct conclusion is to say that neither of them provides any evidence against the hypothesis that we are testing.

If we next turn to point A, we would feel much less confident in asserting that it came from this population. It is not impossible, because the theoretical range of the normal Distribution is unlimited, but it certainly seems very implausible. Much the same can be said of point E, although this is not quite as extreme. This leaves point D to be considered. This is obviously not in a region where values commonly occur, but neither is it extreme enough for us to be confident that it could not have come from this population.

This very informal analysis is sufficient to make the point that there is no clear cut-off point which separates values which are consistent with the hypothesis from those that are not. What we need, therefore, is some means of expressing the uncertainty which we inevitably feel in the situation in which we have been placed.

Before moving on to the next stage of the argument it is worth pausing to notice that we are used to meeting this situation in everyday affairs, although it is often so informal or subconscious that we hardly recognise it. Consider the following situation. We are all aware that people vary in height and we see many examples each day. We carry around in our heads something akin to the frequency distribution of height, although it may be so vague that it seems somewhat extravagant to dignify it by such a term. Nevertheless, we have an intuitive idea of what is 'usual' against which we assess particular cases. Most of the time we do not consciously register this, but every now and again we see someone who is so tall that we do note the fact, and maybe comment on it. We might remark that such and such a person is very tall, or perhaps exceptionally tall. In expressing such judgements we are doing much the same thing as we were doing when comparing points such as A and B in our example, where A was more extreme than B – and similarly in other cases. There is no absolute definition of what 'tall' means, and different people may have different ideas about it. Nevertheless, we all make judgements similar to those we made concerning A and B and the other points, whether or not we recognise the fact. The question for us now is whether we can refine this thinking to provide a useful tool of uncertain inference or, in this particular case, hypothesis testing.

The natural place to begin is to ask whether there is a way to draw a line beyond which we shall declare the hypothesis to be untenable. This may be a natural step but it is fraught with difficulty and has led to much confusion and controversy within the statistical community. We must therefore be clearer about our objective.

It may help if we think of two persons involved in interpreting the result: the 'investigator' and the 'decision-maker'. In many cases these may be one and the same person, but it is convenient to separate the two stages. The role of the investigator is to present the result in terms which make clear where the observed value occurs in relation to the hypothesis being tested. The second person, the decision-maker, then has to decide what to do. In the present example, where we happen to be dealing with a Normal distribution, this is a relatively straightforward matter. If we consider the point D in Figure 8.1, we might note that it is at a distance of twice the standard deviation above the average, and this would tell a person familiar with the Normal distribution exactly where it was. But because we shall not always be dealing with Normal distributions we need an alternative method which is not 'distribution-specific'. One possibility is to specify its location by quoting the proportion of the distribution which lies above, or alternatively below, D. In fact, this is the usual convention and this area, usually expressed as a percentage, is called the *P-value*, or sometimes the *significance level* or, in a broader context, the *Type I error probability*. This is calculable for any distribution and so can be quoted whatever that distribution. If it is very small it means that the observed value is far out in the tail. The farther it is out, the less confident we shall be in asserting that the value comes from this distribution. We have used the word *significance* here in a special sense. In ordinary speech the word is used more generally in a less exact way. When used in this book, as in Statistics generally, it always has this special meaning.

There is one important point we have overlooked in this analysis which is brought out in Figure 8.2. Our lack of confidence will not depend on how far out in the tail, to the right, the observation occurs – what matters is its 'distance' from the centre. Thus an extreme point on the left-hand side will count against the hypothesis just as much as one the same distance on the right. This has been illustrated in Figure 8.2 by 'wrapping round' the distribution illustrated in Figure 8.1. We have to imagine the half of the distribution to the left of the average, equal to 6 here, folded over to lie on top of the right-hand half. In Figure 8.2, therefore, the horizontal axis now represents the distance of the point from the average, and so the values A and B of Figure 8.1 now appear at the appropriate distance from zero.

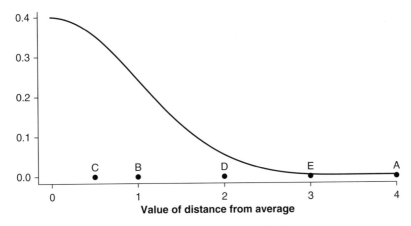

Figure 8.2 'Wrapped round' version of Figure 8.1

When computing the area beyond a point such as D we therefore have to add in the corresponding area of the point the same distance on the other side, that is, two standard deviations below the average. This makes it clear why the sort of test we have been describing is often called a 'two-tailed' test. It is because we are interested only in the distance of a point from the average. The *P*-value of the point D is thus obtained by combining the two tail areas on the right and left to give, approximately, $2 \times 0.025 = 0.05$ because the proportion of the Normal distribution which lies beyond two standard deviations from the average is about 0.05. In practice many statistical tables anticipate this need by giving both of what are called one- and two-tail levels.

Many distinguished statisticians, Sir Ronald Fisher among them, have thought that the statistician's responsibility goes no farther than that of the investigator. They would argue that the scientist's role is to report what has been found. If any decision is called for, it is for others to make it on the basis of the evidence. It would be premature, especially so early in our development of the ideas of Statistics, to prejudge this matter, so we leave it and now turn to the role of the decision-maker.

The question, we recall, is whether we should reject the hypothesis which says that what we have observed was a single observation drawn at random from a specified distribution. Suppose a definite decision has to be made on this evidence alone. There are certainly many practical situations where this applies. They arise, for example, in an examination or testing situation where a candidate needs to reach a given standard in order to proceed. A decision has to be made, and, once made, is final. The question we then face is where to draw the line between 'passing' and 'failing' scores. An obvious way to proceed is to draw a line somewhat arbitrarily and to examine the consequences. The line can then be adjusted in the light of these consequences to obtain a more satisfactory outcome.

Suppose, for the sake of argument, we were to agree to reject the Normal hypothesis, which we have been considering, whenever we observe a value at least 3 standard deviations distant from the average. On this reckoning, observations in the positions of A and E in Figures 8.1 and 8.2 would lead to rejection. To help us judge whether this is a good place to draw the line, let us examine some of the consequences of doing so. The proportion of observations falling beyond this point, which we may interpret as the chance of doing so, for which we shall reject the hypothesis is the area under the curve outside these limits, and this turns out to be 0.0027. This is very small indeed, so it is extremely unlikely that we shall reject the hypothesis when it is true – which is a good thing. However, the farther out we move this limit the more likely it is that we shall fail to detect that the distribution is something different from that under test – which is a bad thing! We are therefore in a position where two opposing risks have to be balanced and any choice will therefore have to be a compromise. How can such a compromise be made when we are trying to balance a known and well-defined risk against something which is more vague? The standard theory of hypothesis testing maintains that the first sort of error, rejecting a hypothesis when it is true, is the more important and that it should be controlled as a matter of first priority. This is analogous to the situation in law where the error of convicting an innocent person is regarded as more serious than failing to convict a guilty person.

These may be unfamiliar ideas, and we shall leave the matter there for the time being and return to them again in the next chapter.

A Second Kind of Inference

The question we have asked so far is: could a given observation have come from a specified population? A second question is: from what populations could this observation have come?

In this form the question is too vague, because the obvious answer is that there is an unlimited number of such populations! To make the question more precise and answerable, we shall have to specify what populations we are willing to entertain. Pending a fuller discussion later, we shall suppose that we only need consider Normal distributions which differ only in their location and hence have the same standard deviation as the one in the example. As before, we suppose that their location is specified by the average and that deviations are measured in multiples of the standard deviation. The position is then as illustrated in Figure 8.3 which we shall use as the basis of our exposition.

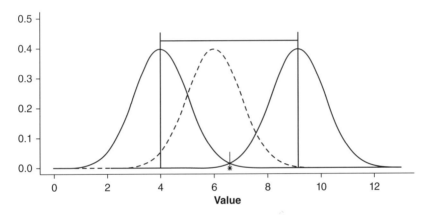

Figure 8.3 Construction of a confidence interval

We start with the point marked by a star on the horizontal axis. This represents the observation. It is located at the value of 6.57, but that number has no essential significance in our argument. If we were testing the hypothesis at the 1% level and using the left-hand distribution, we would just reject that hypothesis because 6.57 corresponds to the 1% point being exactly 2.57 standard deviations above the average. Equally, if we were testing the hypothesis represented by the right-hand distribution, this hypothesis would also be rejected, at the same level, because the starred value is the same distance below the average of that distribution. Any hypothesised distribution with an average farther to the left or the right of the two distributions in Figure 8.3 would certainly be rejected, at that level, because the starred value will be even farther from their respective averages. However, we would fail to reject any distribution which was less extreme. One example of such a distribution is shown on Figure 8.3 by the dashed curve. If that were the true distribution, the starred observation would not be within the limits for rejection. In fact, the value supposed to have been observed is quite close to the average of that distribution. The horizontal line at the top of the diagram spans the averages of all the distributions which would be judged to be within the limits for non-rejection. This interval is called a *confidence interval* and it has associated with it a *confidence coefficient* which, in this case, is 0.99, or 99%. This means that there is a 99% chance that it will include the 'true' value of the average, though that interpretation is not immediately apparent from our analysis. It must await further discussion in Chapter 9.

9

SAMPLING DISTRIBUTIONS AND MORE ON INFERENCE

Summary

In this chapter the basic ideas of inference are extended to include those of a test statistic and its sampling distribution. These ideas are applied, in particular, to the average, where the tendency to Normality is demonstrated. Examples are given of the sampling distribution of the variance and standard deviation. A distinction is drawn between hypothesis testing and estimation.

Introduction

The inference problem as treated in the previous chapter was unrealistic in two respects. First, we supposed that we had a single observation, whereas in almost all inference problems we have a random sample. Therefore, we bypassed entirely the question of how to deal with a sample instead of a single observation. Secondly, the frequency distribution from which we supposed the sample to have been randomly drawn was simply described as 'specified'. No hint was given as to where this distribution might have come from and hence how this distribution might have been specified. In this chapter we shall rectify these omissions and give a more complete account of inference. This will be facilitated if we first define the meaning of key terms.

Hypothesis: A statistical hypothesis is any statement about a frequency distribution. Thus, for example, it may say that its average is 24 and that its form is exponential, or that the proportion of the distribution which is greater than twice its average is 30%, say.

Statistic: This term is the singular of the subject Statistics and it is often used colloquially to refer to a single number, rather as the plural is used to refer to a set of numbers. In statistical inference, however, it means any quantity calculated from a sample. The sample average is thus an example of a statistic, as also are the standard deviation and the proportion of the members of a sample with a value greater than the average. In practice, of course, a statistic is calculated with some particular purpose in view. When that purpose is to make a test of some kind it will often be referred to as a *test statistic.*

Sampling distribution: When making a test we compare the observed value of the test statistic with some distribution. That distribution relates to the test statistic which would result from drawing repeated random samples from some specified distribution and constructing its frequency distribution. A test is thus made in exactly the way described in the last chapter, with the statistic in the role of the 'observed value' and the sampling distribution taking the place of the 'specified distribution'. Notice that another distribution has appeared in the discussion above, and this is the frequency distribution of the original observations. In practice this may be known, either exactly or to a good approximation, or it may be completely unknown.

Standard error: This is the name given to the standard deviation of the sampling distribution. The name is particularly apt in that context because it serves as a measure of the error to which the statistic is subject. There appears to be no special term for the variance of the sampling distribution, so we shall simply refer to it as the *sampling variance.*

The reader should be aware of the way in which the sampling distribution is both like and unlike the distributions we have already met. It is unlike those distributions because it does not exist somewhere in the world waiting to be observed, but is something we have to bring into existence. It only exists after we create it. The principle of the idea can be seen in the example of the Times(1) data used in Chapter 7. There we considered a highly simplified situation in which random samples were being drawn from a population of only 6 sentences, denoted by A, B, ..., F. Suppose we were to draw samples of size 3 as we did there. For example, the first might be ADF and the second BEF. The letters denote values of members of the population which in these cases gives samples with members (27, 15, 38) and (23, 21, 38). If we were interested in the sampling distribution of the average we would calculate the averages for these two samples and then continue in the same way for all subsequent samples. The result of this exercise would be a sequence of averages beginning 26.7, 27.3 and so on. The frequency distribution of the resulting averages would be the *sampling distribution.* In general we would draw many samples of a given size and construct their frequency distribution. The larger the number of samples, the better the sampling distribution will be defined. Historically the method of finding sampling distributions has usually been to use probability theory instead of random sampling, but the results are equivalent. In the easy cases this could be done exactly, but more often it used to be necessary to devise approximations or evaluate complicated mathematical expressions. In many cases the results were set out once and for all in statistical tables which needed to be on hand to any statistician making tests. Nowadays, high-speed computing has rendered all this labour obsolete, in principle at least, and we can, and shall, obtain sampling distributions empirically, from first principles, by repeated sampling from the population distribution. Hereafter we shall be making many statements about distributions, and it is important to distinguish sampling distributions from the frequency distributions of the underlying variable and to be quite clear which is meant.

The greater part of the previous chapter was concerned with testing hypotheses. The second form of inference, discussed at the end of the last chapter, will also be covered here, but only after we have considered its nature more carefully.

Sampling Distribution of the Average

The average is the most important statistic considered in inference, and, with only a brief exception at the end, will be the subject of the remainder of this chapter. The sampling distribution of the average turns out to have some remarkable properties which we shall demonstrate empirically. We would expect the form of the sampling distribution of the average to depend both on the form of the distribution from which the samples are taken and on the size of the sample. The intuitive idea behind the average is that the bigger the sample we take, the better idea we shall get of the variable since the process of averaging should 'iron out' the variation associated with individual values. In other words, we should expect the dispersion of the distribution of an average to decrease as the sample size increases. An important question is how much we gain by increasing the sample size. Just how much improvement we get remains to be seen. We would also expect the averaging to have no effect on the location of the sampling distribution, and this is reflected in the following calculations. All the populations have been chosen to have an average at zero and the sampling distributions follow suit.

In Figures 9.1–9.3 we shall present sampling distributions of the average for different population distributions and varying sample sizes. We begin with samples from a Normal population, shown in Figure 9.1.

It is important to notice that the vertical scale has been varied, as before, to make the change in shape clearer. In reality the total frequency is the same for each distribution. However, the two aspects which we want to compare are the shape and the dispersion. Regarding these two features, it appears from Figure 9.1 that the Normal shape is retained as we form larger samples but the variance diminishes, as we anticipated. In order to see whether these characteristics persist if we change the form of the distribution from which we are sampling, we have repeated these simulations for the rectangular and exponential distributions in Figures 9.2 and 9.3, respectively. The rectangular distribution is symmetrical, like the Normal, but the exponential is highly skewed. It is interesting to see how the behaviour of the sampling distribution depends on the form of the distribution from which we are sampling.

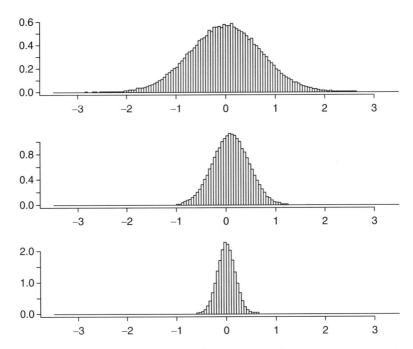

Figure 9.1 Sampling distribution of the average for a Normal population, with sample size 2 (top), 8 (middle) and 32 (bottom)

To facilitate comparison with the results for the Normal distribution we have used, in Figure 9.2, a rectangle with range from −1.732 to +1.732. A uniform distribution with this range has the same average and variance as the Normal with which it is being compared. Once again the dispersion decreases as the sample size is increased, but the distribution is not always Normal in form.

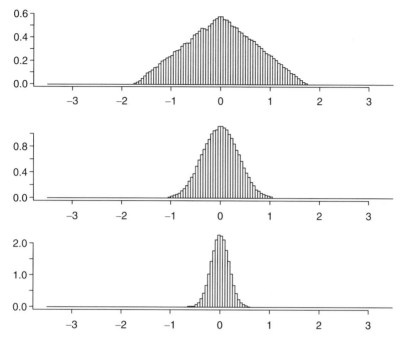

Figure 9.2 Sampling distribution of the average for a rectangular population, with sample size 2 (top), 8 (middle) and 32 (bottom)

This time it appears that the distribution becomes more nearly Normal as the sample size is increased. The same phenomenon is observed when we come to sampling from an exponential distribution, as shown in Figure 9.3.

Here there is a marked skewness of the sampling distribution when the sample size is only 2, but the tendency to Normality becomes apparent for the larger sample sizes. This is not the first time we have met something like this. Something similar occurred in Chapter 3, where the result was illustrated in Figures 3.4 and 3.5 for two and three components. However, in that case we were dealing with sums rather than averages and we were not dealing with sampling distributions. These examples show that the tendency to Normality is a characteristic of the averaging process and suggests that what we have observed for these particular distributions may be true for all distributions. This is where mathematics could demonstrate its power by establishing that what we have found in these particular distributions is also true of almost all other distributions. The reduction in dispersion which we have also noted is not merely qualitative but can take a rather special form, as Table 9.1 shows. This table gives the calculated standard errors of the sampling distributions for different sample sizes.

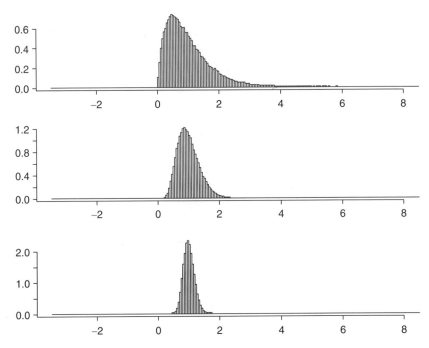

Figure 9.3 Sampling distribution of the average for an exponential population, with sample size 2 (top), 8 (middle) and 32 (bottom)

Table 9.1 Standard error related to sample size for three distributions

Sample size	2	8	32
Normal	0.705	0.353	0.177
Rectangular	0.707	0.353	0.177
Exponential	0.706	0.353	0.176

For all practical purposes the rows of this table are identical. It must be remembered that these numbers will vary slightly from one simulation to another, but we have deliberately made the number of replications large enough for the variation to be negligible. Furthermore, what we have found for these three distributions is true for all others. Expressed in words, what we have discovered is that you have to quadruple the sample size to halve the standard error. There is thus a kind of law of diminishing returns which operates in sampling. The larger the sample you have, the larger any increment needs to be to obtain an equivalent reduction in standard error. Table 9.1 also shows why we chose those particular sample sizes in the simulations. It was in anticipation of the quadrupling rule that we constructed this particular example.

It must be remembered that all of the foregoing relates to averages. These are certainly the most important statistics we encounter, but it should not be assumed that all sampling distributions are Normal – at least if the sample size is large enough. This is a question which we must leave open, but there is one other statistic where it will be useful to know something about its sampling distribution. This is the variance or, equivalently, the standard deviation.

Sampling Distribution of the Variance

We now give examples of some further sampling distributions when sampling from a Normal distribution. These are of the variance and the standard deviation. The reason for this is twofold. First, it will give the reader further experience of sampling distributions and prepare the ground for a more complete account of hypothesis testing. Secondly, and more immediately, it will be useful to know something about the variation of these two statistics when we come to the tests of the next chapter. In Figure 9.4 we give examples of the sampling distributions of the variance for two different sample sizes, 10 and 100. This shows that with a sample of 10 the sample variance varies a good deal. Although its average is close to 1, as we would expect, it varies over a wide range. Thus it would be perfectly possible to obtain a sample variance close to zero or as large as 2 or, even 3. By the time the sample size is increased to 100 the sampling distribution is much more tightly clustered around 1 and is also nearly symmetrical.

In Figure 9.5 we look at the sampling distribution of the standard deviation when the sample is drawn from a Normal distribution. The latter choice is the one most relevant for later purposes. The upper and lower parts of this figure show the effect of increasing the sample size. In both cases the form of the distribution is more symmetrical than it was for the variance, but the tenfold change in sample size produces a marked reduction in dispersion. In the latter case the sample standard deviation is much closer to the expected value of 1, implying that the sample standard deviation is quite a good estimate of the true value when the sample size is of this order.

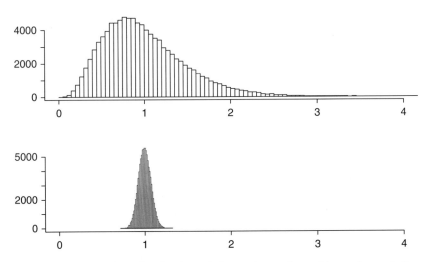

Figure 9.4 Sampling distribution of the variance for a Normal population, with sample size 10 (top) and 100 (bottom)

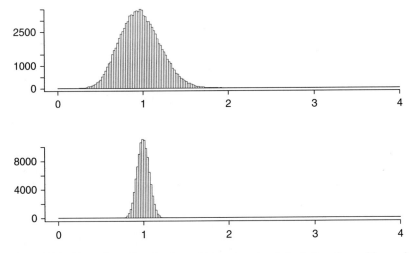

Figure 9.5 Sampling distribution of the standard deviation for a Normal population, with sample size 10 (top) and 100 (bottom)

Figure 9.5, incidentally, illustrates another point which we made earlier when discussing the effect of transformations on the form of the distribution. The standard deviation is the square root of the variance, and we note here that this transformation has had the effect of making the form of the distribution more nearly Normal. One potential consequence of this is that there might be an advantage in using the standard deviation when making inferences about the population dispersion because any assumption about its Normality might be easier to justify.

Note on the Determination of Sampling Distributions

All of the above sampling distributions have been determined from first principles in the sense that we have actually drawn a very large number of random samples from the specified distribution, calculated the statistic and then constructed a histogram of the distribution. That is why the distributions look like histograms, albeit with such large frequencies that their outlines strongly suggested a smooth curve. In the earlier part of this book, when talking about population distributions, we used smooth curves as an indication of the shape to which the empirical distribution seemed to be tending and thus regarded it, in a sense, as an approximation to the continuous form. For example, in Chapter 2 the emphasis was on the 'shape' of the distributions and this was most simply expressed by drawing smooth curves. In the present case, we wish to emphasise the method by which the distribution is constructed as well as the resulting shape. As mentioned at the beginning of this chapter, the traditional way of finding sampling distributions is using probability theory, and we could have used established results for the standard cases we have considered and plotted curves accordingly. We have preferred the empirical approach because it is universally applicable whether or not it might have been possible to calculate sampling distributions theoretically. By using large samples of size 100,000 we have been able to attain sufficient precision to show distributions which are smooth enough for all practical purposes yet without needing any theoretical support. Any of these distributions can be obtained in a minute or two on a standard laptop computer, and so it is arguable that theoretical methods, on which universal reliance has hitherto been placed, are now obsolete.

Inference Continued

We are now in a position to bring the ingredients of a statistical inference problem together and give a more complete account of hypothesis testing. It will now be clear why, in the last chapter, we used a Normal distribution as the basis of the exposition. This was because many sampling distributions are either exactly Normal in form, or close to it. The second aspect of a hypothesis testing problem was the test statistic. Purely for simplicity of the exposition in the previous chapter, we treated this as a single observation. Now we must be more specific. In all of the problems we shall meet at the present level, the choice seems so obvious that it hardly merits discussion. For example, if we are interested in the average of a population it seems natural to take the sample average as a test statistic and ask what we can infer about the population average from it. This is the case with all the examples we shall meet in this book, but it is worth pointing out that the choice is not always so obvious and a major part of the theory of statistical inference is about finding an appropriate statistic in such cases.

We continue our account of inference by returning to the case of the average. We now know that the sampling distribution of the average is either exactly Normal or, if the sample size is sufficiently large, approximately Normal. Furthermore, we have a good idea of how large the sample has to be to justify the assumption of Normality. Under these circumstances it might seem that the previous chapter provides all that we need to go ahead and make inferences about the population average. However, there is one crucial difference which prevents us from taking the easy course. Everything in the previous chapter supposed that the variance of what we may now call the sampling distribution was known. This may not be immediately apparent because there we supposed that the scale of the Normal distribution was measured in units of its standard deviation. This amounts to supposing that we know what that unit is. We can therefore only make use of these ideas if we know the standard deviation of the population from which the sample has been drawn. There are examples, mainly in the physical sciences, where we have a very good idea what this variance may be. Thus if the variation arises as an error of measurement, that variation depends primarily on the measuring instrument, and this may be known from long experience. The average, on the other hand, arises from the thing being measured and it is this which is unknown. It is hard to find similar examples in the social sciences and so it may seem that we have an insuperable problem since we are supposedly in the situation of not knowing the average but needing to know the variance. It thus seems that we can only buy knowledge about one unknown at the price of assuming a value for another! The way out of this dilemma lies in the fact that, although we do not know the variance, we can obtain an estimate of it. Using this estimate is not simply a matter of inserting this estimate in place of the unknown quantity but involves a more fundamental approach which we shall expound in the next chapter. For the moment, to round off our account, we shall simply assume, quite unrealistically, that the variance of the population sampled is known.

Under these circumstances the hypothesis testing problem has, indeed, already been solved as in the previous chapter. We shall, however, return to the estimation problem which was covered at the end of that chapter. It was pointed out there that it was possible to construct an interval which we described as a confidence interval for the unknown average. Here we take that argument farther by justifying, more adequately, the use of that term.

Inference is commonly described as falling into two parts: hypothesis testing and estimation. The estimation problem is split into two parts called *point estimation* and *interval estimation*. The former is concerned with obtaining the best single number which can stand for the unknown being estimated. At the elementary level this seems almost self-evident – the sample average, for example, is the obvious quantity to take as the point estimate of the population average. An interval estimate, as its name implies, is an interval within which we confidently expect the true value to lie. A method of obtaining such an interval for an unknown population average was given at the end of Chapter 8. Here we extend that argument to show how we may attach a probability to such an interval.

The method depends on the logical equivalence of the following statements:

1. The chance that the difference between the sample average and the population average is more than two standard errors is approximately 5%.
2. The chance that the sample average is more than two standard errors from the population average is 5%.
3. The chance that the population average is more than two standard errors from the sample average is 5%.
4. The chance that the population average is less than two standard errors from the sample average is 95%.

The last statement specifies what is called a 95% confidence interval for the population average.

We have chosen 'two standard errors' because it so happens that this is associated with a probability of 95%, but there is no loss of generality in substituting other distances and probabilities. For example, 1.65 standard errors is associated with a probability of 90%. These two examples correspond to significance levels of 5% and 10%, respectively.

Non-Normal Sampling Distributions

Many of the arguments used above depend on the assumption of a Normal sampling distribution. But we know from the distribution of the sample variance shown in Figure 9.4 that sampling distributions do not necessarily have this form. Sometimes it is still a fairly straight-forward matter to extend the argument to non-Normal distributions, and we shall give an example in a moment. However, it is important to emphasise that, knowing the sampling distribution, it is always possible to say something useful about the plausibility of a particular hypothesis. For example, the sampling distribution in Figure 9.4 tells us, if the true variance is 1 for sampling from a Normal distribution, something about what values are likely to occur. If the sample size is around 10 the range of possibilities is very large, from close to zero to upwards of 2.5. Increasing the sample size to 100, the range is much narrower and we would be surprised to find anything much outside the range (0.8, 1.25), say. Although statements like this lack the precision of formal test results, they are far better than the ill-considered judgements of those unfamiliar with the notion of sampling variability.

If we know that our sample came from a particular distribution, such as the Normal, we can carry out a test on the same lines as we used for the average. We would still want to reject our hypothesis if the observed deviation from expectation was too large in either direction. This can be achieved by drawing a pair of lines, as in Figure 9.6, which, together, cut off a specified percentage of the sampling distribution. This has been done in Figure 9.6 in such a way that 5% of the distribution lies outside them. If an observed value of the sample variance were in this region we would be justified in rejecting the hypothesis that the population variance was 1. The rejection region has been divided into two equal parts of 2.5% each. This implies that the importance of any given deviation from what is expected, is judged by the proportion of the distribution lying beyond this point rather than by its distance from the average. Put in another way, we are saying that we attach more importance to a deviation of a given magnitude if it is below the average than if it is above it. This reflects the fact that the distribution is skewed in a way that makes big deviations above the average relatively more common than below the average.

We could calculate a P-value above the average by finding the proportion of the distribution lying above it and then doubling the quantity because an equivalent deviation below the average would count equally against the hypothesis. Conversely, an observed value below the average contributes two tail areas to the *P*-value. It is common to find the significance of a result expressed in the form *P* < 0.05, say. This is because many published tables of sampling distributions only give a few values corresponding to commonly used significance levels. One advantage of generating sampling distributions empirically is that more exact values can always be found. Obtaining things like confidence intervals for quantities such as the variance with skewed sampling distributions is possible, but they require a slightly broader framework than the one we have adopted and are not dealt with here.

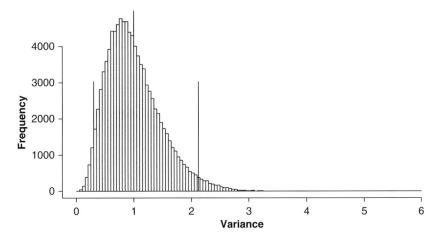

Figure 9.6 Sampling distribution of the variance showing the average and upper and lower 2.5% cut-offs

10

INFERENCE ABOUT AVERAGES

Summary

This chapter deals with the standard test situations which arise when comparing averages with variance known or unknown. However, the test statistics are slightly simpler than those which are in common use because the sampling distributions are obtained directly by empirical means. Examples of the sampling distributions for comparing several averages are given.

Introduction

This title links the subject firmly to traditional treatments of the subject. In the present context we might equally have spoken of inference about Normal distributions with known variance. This would have linked it more clearly with Chapter 5 on the analysis of variation of which it is, in many ways, a continuation. In that chapter we were asking whether we could decompose a given distribution into parts, the existence of which, in an obvious sense, would explain the original variation. The whole thrust in Chapter 5 hinged on examining whether the variation between the subgroups was greater than would be expected on the evidence of the variation within subgroups. We now ask similar questions, but with the possibility of answering them by reference to sampling variation arising from the fact that we are dealing with random samples. We begin with the simplest case where there is only one sample to consider, and then move on to two samples and then more than two, when the affinity with the subject of Chapter 5 will be more obvious.

Inference from a Single Sample

Here the situation is the same as that in the previous chapter, but with the crucial difference that the standard deviation of the population is unknown. In Chapter 9 we showed that inference could be based on the distance of the sample average from the population average, measured in units of the standard error. For example, if the sample average differed from the population average by more than twice the standard error we could reasonably conclude, at a specified level of significance, 5% in that example, that the sample was unlikely to have come from a Normal population with that average. But if the population standard deviation is unknown, we cannot do this and may feel that we have reached an impasse. The obvious solution is to replace the unknown standard deviation by an estimate, which we could certainly obtain from the sample before us. However, this estimate will vary from one sample to another and this implies that a confidence interval, for example, will vary in length. This means that it will sometimes stand a better chance of 'catching' the true value and sometimes a worse one. It is not at all clear how things will 'balance out'. A better way is to recognise that the sampling distribution will not be the same when the estimated standard error takes the place of the true value. Starting from this fact, we can proceed in exactly the same way as before but using the true sampling distribution and so obtain a valid inference.

In principle there is no problem in obtaining the required sampling distribution, since this can always be done empirically by actual sampling. This is what we shall do. Instead of looking at the deviation measured in units of the actual standard error, we shall do so in terms of the estimated standard error.

It will be useful to pose the testing question we are asking in terms which make a stronger link with our earlier exposition of inference but also, more importantly, which will prepare the ground for the relatively more complicated problems which arise when there are several averages involved. To carry out a test we first require a suitable test statistic, and then we need to know its sampling distribution. In the case of a single average with known standard error, we carried out the test by calculating how far the average was from its expectation in multiples of the standard error. This could then be compared with the standard Normal sampling distribution in order to judge its significance. This procedure is exactly equivalent to first dividing the average by its standard error and then referring the result to the standard Normal distribution. It is this version which lends itself to the extension we are now contemplating.

The only difference is that the population standard deviation, which is an essential part of the standard error, is unknown. All that has to be done is to replace the unknown standard deviation by an estimate obtained from the sample. This yields the required test statistic which, we repeat, is the sample average divided by the estimated standard error. The one thing lacking now is the sampling distribution of this test statistic. We can find out what this is by determining the sampling distribution empirically. This has been done, and the result is presented in Figure 10.1, when the sample size is 10 and the number of samples is 100,000. This number of samples has been used in all our examples.

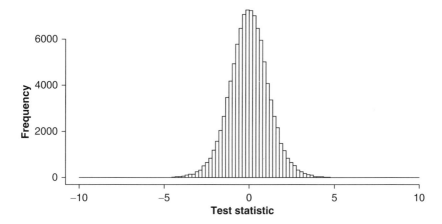

Figure 10.1 Sampling distribution of a test statistic for a test on a single mean, with sample size 10

At first sight this looks just like a Normal distribution, but it is certainly not the standard Normal distribution we would expect if substituting the estimated standard error had made no difference. This is most easily seen by noticing that the standard deviation of this distribution is not 1. To make a wider point, the standard deviations of the sampling distribution are given in Table 10.1 for a variety of sample sizes.

Table 10.1 Standard errors for the sampling distribution of the test statistic illustrated in Figure 10.1

Sample size	100	50	10
Standard error	1.02	1.03	1.19

It is clear that this sampling distribution has a larger dispersion than the standard Normal distribution, but that the difference diminishes as the sample size increases. It is thus only for small sample sizes, of the order of 10, say, that it is important to take account of the sample size. To make the point in another way, if we were to observe an estimated value of 1.7 we could calculate, from the empirical sampling distribution, that the proportion of the sampling distribution below that point was 7%, so the proportion that far from zero in either direction would be 14%. Hence there would be little prospect that such a difference would be regarded as significant. However, if the estimated standard error was actually the true value, the corresponding proportion would have been about 4.4%, or 8.8% taking both tails. This is considerably less than the 14% of the former case.

A confidence interval can also be constructed, and when we are interested only in a single average this is likely to be of greater practical interest. When the standard error was known, the 95% confidence interval extended a distance of 2 standard errors on either side of the average. To turn this into a confidence interval when the standard error has to be estimated, we replace the known population standard deviation by the estimated value and the 2 by the corresponding value for the relevant sampling distribution as given by Figure 10.1. In the latter case we require the point beyond which 2.5% of the empirical distribution lies. This turns out to be 2.376, which is larger than the 2 we used before. In general, therefore, the confidence interval will be longer when the standard error has to be estimated, as we would expect. The qualification 'in general' is important because it could happen that we had a substantial underestimate of the standard error, in which case the interval could, actually, be shorter. The important point to notice is that the length of the interval varies from sample to sample and is not fixed as it was in the Normal case. When we say that it has a certain chance of including the true value we are really making an 'average' statement which, we have to imagine, is derived from an indefinitely large number of random samples. We are not saying, as people tend to suppose, that this particular interval has the specified chance, in some sense, of including the true value. This feature is seen by some as a disadvantage of confidence intervals, but it seems unavoidable if we choose to base inferences on sampling distributions.

Before moving on to the case of two averages, we mention a problem which is sometimes wrongly mistaken for a 'two-average' problem but is, in fact, a 'one- average' problem handled by the approach given above.

It is common to take what we might call 'before' and 'after' measurements on the same sample member. For example, we might make measurements of the degree of memory recall before and after the administration of a drug to a sample of subjects. Our interest is then in whether the drug has an effect on how much subjects can recall. The difference between the 'after' and 'before' measurements is then a reasonable measure of the effect of the drug. There is thus a single measure of effect which happens to have been obtained in two parts. Any test or estimate of effectiveness of the drug is thus based on one sample of individuals and a 'one-sample' method is therefore appropriate.

Comparison of Two Samples

Following the general pattern for constructing tests of significance, we start by devising a suitable test statistic and then generating its sampling distribution empirically. An obvious test statistic in this case is the difference between the averages of the separate samples. If we remind ourselves that we are really testing the difference between two distributions, and therefore using their averages as convenient summary measures, this implies that we are assuming the two populations to have the same variance. By assuming also that the samples have come from Normal populations, we know that the sampling variance of the difference will be the sum of the corresponding values for the two samples. Because we do not know this variance, we shall follow the precedent adopted in the case of one sample, replacing it by the sample variance. All that remains to be done before we can carry out the test is to construct the empirical sampling distribution. This is done by drawing a very large number of pairs of samples at random from the same Normal distribution and constructing the frequency distribution of the test statistic. An example is provided in Figure 10.2.

This turns out to very similar in shape to that given in Figure 10.1 for the case of a single sample. In fact, it may be shown mathematically that the form is identical – in this case depending only on the sum of the two sample sizes.

This is a good place to introduce the distinction between one- and two-tailed tests since the need for both commonly arises when comparing two averages. If, for example, we were comparing the effect of a new drug on two randomly chosen groups of subjects, we may know that the new drug can only have a beneficial effect and hence that the only real differences in response will be those which attribute a larger response to the new drug. Alternatively, we may only be interested in differences in one direction. In either case we shall only wish to attribute significance to differences in a particular direction. In our original treatment of tests of significance it was the distance of the test statistic from expectation which mattered so both tails of the sampling distribution were relevant. For the example envisaged here, it is the distance in only one direction that counts against the hypothesis under test. Consequently the *P*-value of the test is the proportion of the sampling distribution lying beyond the observed value which we need. For a two-tailed test we would have doubled this tail proportion.

We can construct a confidence interval for the difference between the two population averages in the usual way, but in practice, and in contrast to the single-sample case, it is the problem of hypothesis testing which usually occurs.

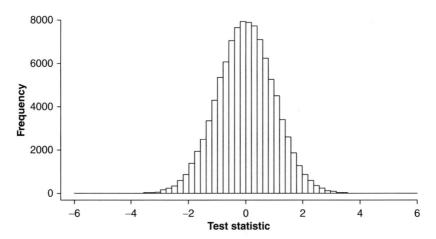

Figure 10.2 Sampling distribution of the test for the difference between two sample means, with sample sizes 10

More than Two Samples

When we move from two to more than two samples we immediately encounter the question of what test statistic to use because there is, at first sight, no obvious statistic equivalent to the difference in averages. We want something which simultaneously measures the difference between a set of several averages. However, we have already met the question of how to measure the variation of a set of numbers, and that is precisely equivalent to what we require here. This analogy is strengthened by recalling that the variance is also an average of the squared differences between all pairs of values. Applying that insight here suggests that the variance of the sample averages about their common average would provide a suitable test statistic. Such a sum of squares would be close to zero if the averages were close together and would increase as they became more distant from one another. All of this is in line with what the analysis of variation, discussed in Chapter 5, would suggest. There we were concerned with the possibility of breaking down a distribution into parts, which we spoke of as the analysis of variation. It is important to notice that by using the variance we have sacrificed being able to distinguish the 'direction' of any difference, as we were able to do using the difference of just two averages.

There also seems to be a question about what to compare the 'between-groups' variance with. In the case of two averages, the obvious thing to do seemed to be to divide the difference in averages by their estimated standard error. In the present case we could, in principle, work out the standard error of the between-groups variance, but we shall follow a simpler course by pursuing the parallel with Chapter 5 further. There the idea was that if the total variation could be broken down into two parts, then the variation between groups should be at least as great as the variation within groups. There are thus two parts which could each be an estimate of the variance in the absence of any difference between the groups. First of all, there is the variation within groups, which we can easily estimate by simply taking the average of the individual group variances. Secondly, there are the group averages. Their variance is easily obtained but we must remember that these averages will necessarily have a smaller variance because we have had to average n original measurements in order to get them. Our estimate of the required variance obtained from them will thus be n times too small and we must therefore multiply it by n to make it comparable with that derived from the within-group variation. We can then compare these two estimates with one another by dividing the former by the latter. This is what we have done when calculating the sampling distribution shown in Figure 10.3. Appropriately, this statistic is called a *variance ratio*.

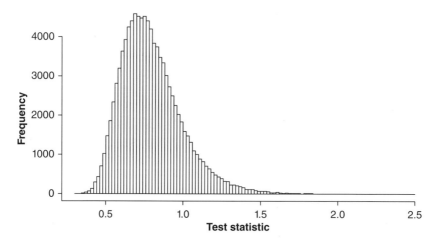

Figure 10.3   Distribution of test statistic for four groups and $n = 10$

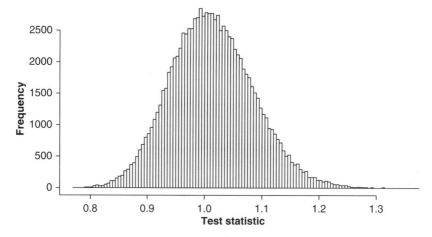

Figure 10.4   Distribution of test statistic for four groups and $n = 100$

There are two novel features about this sampling distribution compared with those we have met before. First, it is asymmetrical – nothing like a Normal distribution. Secondly, we are only interested in significance in the upper tail. In fact, very small values of the statistic would indicate that there is much less variation between groups than we would expect. Evidence of real differences between groups is provided by large values of the statistic, so we shall only judge significance in the upper tail.

If we increase the size of the groups, the shape of the distribution does not greatly change, as we see from Figure 10.4, where there is still some skewness. In both cases the value 1, which corresponds to the case when the two estimates of variance are equal, occurs in the central part of the distribution.

The Assumptions

The ability to find sampling distributions empirically and very quickly means that we can introduce other important ideas in Statistics, even though it is not possible to pursue them in depth. In the remainder of this chapter we shall therefore introduce two of these.

The perceptive reader may have noticed that we have had to make assumptions about the form of the population from which our sample has been drawn. Up to this point the assumption has usually been that the form of the distribution was Normal. In most cases there seems to have been little evidence for this assumption, and the reader may have noticed that, in most cases, we cannot even know what that distribution is! What, then, is the justification, beyond convenience, for this assumption? When confronted with this awkward question statisticians have pursued two lines of defence. The first is by discovering whether the assumptions matter very much. For if they play little role in the determination of sampling distributions, it hardly matters what assumptions we make. Statistical procedures which are insensitive to the underlying assumptions are called *robust*. The study of robustness is an important branch of statistical research and, fortunately, many commonly used procedures are robust. This feature is illustrated in Figure 10.5 for the case of the test that two distributions have the same average, but this is only an illustration, of course!

The top distribution is equivalent to the one shown in Figure 10.2. The middle and lower distributions are for two highly non-Normal distributions. The one in the middle is for a uniform distribution which, though symmetrical like the Normal distribution, has no tails at all. The bottom distribution is for the exponential distribution, which is very highly skewed. The remarkable thing about this comparison is that all three sampling distributions are very similar. In part, we may surmise, this is because a common feature is that all involve a difference in averages for samples of size 10 and we already know that averages have approximately Normal distributions, but this is not true of the measures of variation which appear in the denominators. As a further means of comparison we have constructed Table 10.2, which shows the standard deviations and the upper 2.5% points and 0.5% points – which are particularly relevant when making tests of significance.

In this case, at least, it appears that the differences are quite small, even in the extreme cases we have considered. It is difficult to conceive of circumstances under which such differences would have serious practical consequences. We may therefore conclude that the two-sample test for averages is robust.

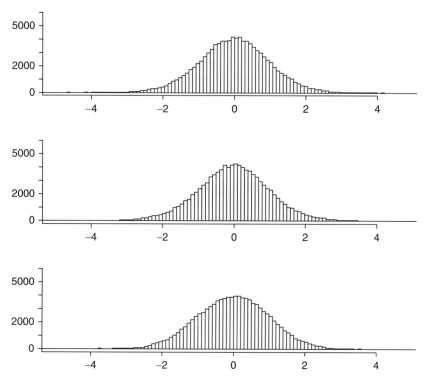

Figure 10.5 Sampling distribution of test statistic when the population distribution is Normal (top), uniform (middle) and exponential (bottom)

Table 10.2 Percentage points for the test comparing two means for various assumptions about the underlying frequency distribution

	Standard deviation	2.5% point	0.5% point
Normal	1.00	2.03	2.70
Uniform	1.01	2.05	2.82
Exponential	1.00	1.95	2.56

The second way of coping with the need to make, possibly unjustified, assumptions, is to use what are called 'distribution-free' tests. As their name implies, these require no assumptions about the underlying frequency distributions of the variable. At first sight this is an attractive way forward and we shall give one or two examples in the next chapter.

However, there are two drawbacks. First, many hypotheses which we may wish to investigate concern properties of the frequency distributions themselves and it is not clear what happens to these if the distributions are swept away. Secondly, there may be a subtle change in the character of the hypotheses which can best be seen when we come to consider particular problems later.

Power

The hypothesis being tested, often called the *null hypothesis*, has a privileged status in the theory of hypothesis testing and the onus is on the data to show that it is false. Often the null hypothesis represents a position from which we are reluctant to depart. For example, if we are testing a new drug there may be many new alternatives which have yet to prove their value. There may also be substantial costs, monetary and otherwise, which make us reluctant to make a change without convincing evidence. At the same time we would not wish to miss the possibility of finding a better alternative if one exists. The ideal test, therefore, will be one which not only makes us reluctant to reject the old but also has a good chance of rejecting the old in favour of something better. Put another way, our test must have a good chance of detecting an improvement if a better drug exists. The capacity of a test to do this is known as its *power*. A powerful test is one which not only controls the chance of wrongly rejecting the null hypothesis but has a good chance of finding a better alternative. The ability to determine sampling distributions empirically makes it as easy to find the power of a test as to find its sampling distribution when the null hypothesis is not true. It is easy to see that we can increase power by increasing sample size, but here we are concerned more with the possibility of comparing tests, and this is most meaningfully done by assuming that the sample size is the same for them all.

We shall therefore illustrate the idea of power using the test for a single average where the data are obtained from a 'before' and 'after' situation. The question is: how likely is it that we shall detect a real difference of a specified magnitude? A convenient way to do this is to measure departures from the hypothesis tested in units of the standard error when it turns out that the power does not depend, additionally, on the sample size, so the comparison we make is independent of sample size. The results of such a comparison are shown in Figure 10.6.

To keep things simple we imagine rejecting the hypothesis tested whenever the test statistic is greater than 2; the chance of so doing is

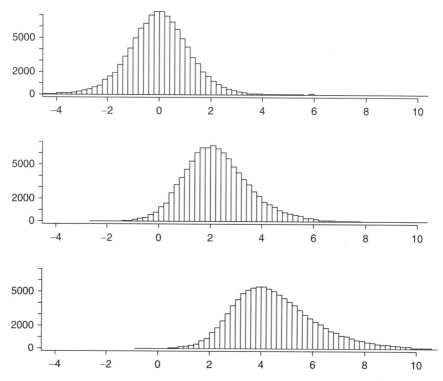

Figure 10.6   Power of the one-sample test for deviations measured in multiples of the standard error, with average 0 (top), 2 (middle) and 4 (bottom)

about 2.5%. If the average is actually 2 standard errors greater than zero, about half of the relevant sampling distribution is greater than 2, whereas in the case of a separation of 4 standard errors, well over 90% of the sampling distribution lies in that region. This is only illustrative, of course, but it shows how modest departures from the hypothesis tested may easily pass undetected.

11

BINARY DATA

Summary

In this chapter, examples are given of binary data coded as a sequence of 0s and 1s and the link is established with quantitative data. The binomial and Poisson distributions are shown to arise by considering the number of 1s in a sequence. The waiting time for the first, or nth, 1 is illustrated as giving rise to the geometric and the negative binomial distributions.

Introduction

Binary data are the simplest kind of statistical data. They record only whether some attribute is present or not. Thus, for example, if an interviewer records whether a call is successful (S) or not (N) the record of successive calls might be as follows:

S, S, N, S, N, S, S, N, N, S, S, N, N, N, …

This is an example of binary data. Similarly, those taking an examination might be recorded as pass or fail, and a sequence of tosses of a coin as heads, tails, heads, tails, tails, tails, and so on. For brevity a single symbol might be used for each outcome, but that does not essentially change anything. The examination results might then appear as P, P, P, F, P, F, P, P, P, and so on. There is nothing to stop us from using numbers instead of letters as codes for the outcomes, but this should not mislead us into thinking of those numbers as magnitudes. No one would make the mistake of interpreting the numbers on the backs of footballers as quantities in any sense; they are simply codes which, with the help of a printed programme, enable us to identify the players.

There is, however, one numerical labelling which does enable us to make the transition from arbitrary symbols to numbers in a useful and meaningful way. Suppose we agree to denote a pass in the examination by 1 and a fail by 0; then the foregoing sequence might be written, 1, 1, 1, 0, 1, 0, 1, 1, 1, ... The advantage of doing this is that, in some important respects, we can carry out arithmetical operations on these symbols just as if they were magnitudes. For example, if we add them up we obtain the total numbers of 1s in the sequence. Building on this simple observation, we can develop a whole range of analyses which closely parallel those given earlier in this book.

Binary variables are also the simplest example of 'discrete' variables which take only particular values; another example is the number of children in a household. They are also the simplest kind of example of a categorical variable which records into which of a number of categories an individual falls. So far we have chosen not to make distinctions in the type of variable, because we have been more concerned to emphasise the patterns of variation through which the basic ideas of Statistics can be expressed most economically. We shall continue on that path by showing how some important aspects of the analysis of binary data fit quite naturally into that earlier framework.

The Binomial Distribution

Our starting point has been the frequency distribution whose visual representation in the form of the histogram provided a readily intelligible picture of the variation. With binary data this representation is almost trivial because there are only two possibilities and the histogram would merely record how many 1s and 0s there are, which does not take us very much farther. However, things become more interesting if we take a further step. The average of any distribution of binary variables is the total number of 1s divided by the total number of cases, which is simply the proportion of 1s. This immediately establishes a link between that proportion and the average of the distribution. We have already met many analyses involving averages, so there is now the prospect that some of these might be appropriate for the proportions which arise with binary data.

The variance, we recall, is obtained by first taking the squared difference between the variable and its average, and then averaging those squares. In the case of binary data there are only two possible values for this difference, which must either be the difference between one and the proportion or the proportion itself. It turns out that this is the same as the average multiplied by the proportion of 0s. It follows from this, incidentally, that the variance is necessarily less than the average.

Armed with these preliminary results, we go on to consider three important distributions associated with binary data and we shall show how they arise. The first concerns the number of 1s and 0s there are in a sample of given size. The total number of 1s, or 0s for that matter, is now of particular interest. For example, it would be the total number in a class who passed the examination or the number of successful calls by the interviewer. This distribution is known as the *binomial* distribution. The shape of the distribution depends both on the proportion of 1s in the population and on the size of the sample that we take. Some examples of the varying shapes of this distribution are given in Figure 11.1. In fact, these are equivalent to sampling distributions because they can be obtained by taking a sample of a given size from an appropriate population. It may also happen that such distributions arise naturally in certain situations. For example, we may classify the adults in households of, say, size 4 as employed or unemployed. If the observed distribution of number employed had the binomial form we would be justified in entertaining the hypothesis that individuals all had an equal chance of being employed. If the distribution was not binomial, we might hope to obtain a clue to the reasons for the inadequate fit. By studying the shape of the binomial distribution we can expect to learn something along these lines.

Note that we have only considered values of the proportion between 0.5 and 1. This is because the 0s and 1s are interchangeable, meaning that the choice of which response is coded 0 and which 1 is entirely arbitrary. The shape of the distribution when the proportion is 0.25 is thus exactly the same as when the proportion is 0.75, for example, apart from the fact that it is reflected from left to right.

Although the number of 1s is always discrete, the discreteness looks increasingly unimportant as the size increases. Apart from this aspect, it is clear that the distribution approaches the Normal form as the size increases when we move down the columns of Figure 11.1. This is true even when the proportion is close to 1, at the right hand of Figure 11.1, but the approach to Normality is then slower. We might have expected this approach to Normality because we are dealing with sums of binary variables. The approach to Normality, however, also depends on the value of the proportion and, as we have just noted, is much slower when it is very small. Figure 11.1 only illustrates this, of course, but what we have found empirically in a few cases is always true.

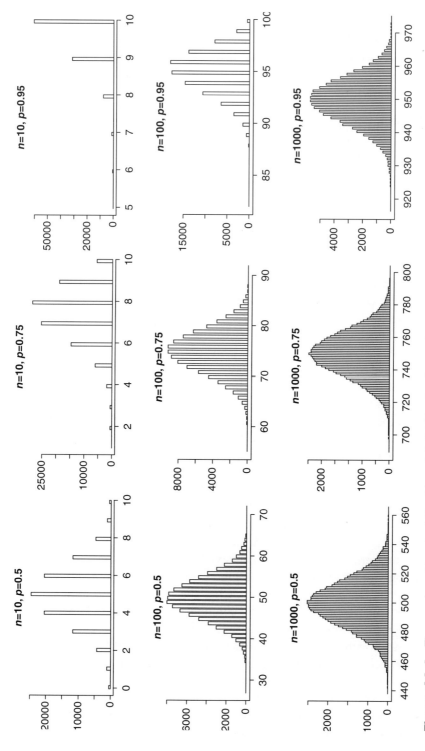

Figure 11.1 The varying shapes of the binomial distribution for various values of the sample size (*n*) and proportion (*p*); the horizontal scale is the number of 1s

Rare Events

The population of the United States of America is over 300 million. If a disease strikes, on average, one person in every million per year, it is certainly a rare disease. Hardly anyone will contract it, even in a lifetime, and it will be something which people rarely encounter. Yet one would expect there to be several hundred cases a year in the whole country. It is something which is extremely rare at an individual level, but quite common nationally. It would thus be considered improvident for national agencies not to fund facilities for its treatment. In practice there are many rare events of this kind, particularly in the realm of accident statistics. Commercial flying may be properly described as extremely safe but there are very many individual flights when an accident might conceivably occur so that, on a worldwide basis the total number of accidents per year, for example, may be far from negligible. Accident statistics often come in the form of binary data where the result of each trial flight, outing, or whatever, is recorded as involving an accident or not. Any record will consist of a very large number of 0s (denoting, let us suppose, non-occurrence) and a small number of 1s. If, as before, we imagine each observation to have been sampled at random from a population with a specified proportion of 1s, we are now in a situation where that proportion is exceedingly small. But if the number of cases is very large the average would be neither very large nor very small. If we now repeat the argument we used to deduce the variance, the amount to be subtracted from the average will become vanishingly small, which makes the variance virtually the same as the average. Thus, whatever the form the distribution turns out to be, it will have an average which is almost the same as the variance. This is an extremely useful property of distributions arising under these circumstances. There is no difficulty in looking at binomial distributions derived by supposing that when the proportions are very small but where the number of cases is large enough for there to be a reasonable number of 1s. Note that we do not need to specify the proportion and the sample size separately: it is sufficient to know their product, the average. Some examples are given in Figure 11.2.

The horizontal axis in each case specifies the number of 1s. The distributions all share the property that the average and variance are equal to the value shown at the head of each diagram. It appears that as the average increases, so does the tendency to Normality – a fact which can be proved. A distribution of this kind is known as a *Poisson* distribution after the distinguished French mathematician of that name.

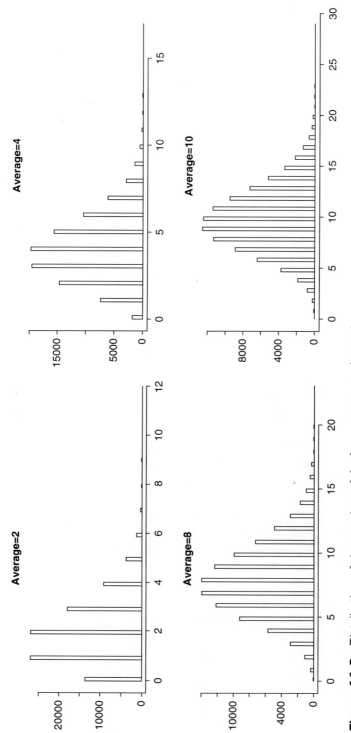

Figure 11.2 Distribution of the number of 1s for rare events for various averages

In practice we may not know exactly what the proportion is or how many cases there are, beyond the fact that it is very large. However, this does not matter because, as we have already noted, all we need to know is the average, which is the product of the two and this is easily estimated from the average of the distribution. We may also be far from certain that the proportions, though small, are all the same. For example, people may vary in their propensity to contract a rare disease. This does not matter either, as long as the risk is very small for all of them.

It often happens that we might expect, or hope, that a distribution would conform to the Poisson shape but in practice it turns out otherwise. In such cases it is usually found that the variance is greater than the average instead of being about the same. The first step is to make sure that the deviation is not simply a sampling variation, and for this we need an appropriate test of significance. One way of doing this is by comparing the average and the variance, because these should be the same if the distribution is Poisson. The next step is to construct a suitable test statistic, which could be the ratio of the variance and the average. We then could determine its sampling distribution empirically from a large number of random samples and then judge whether the deviation of the value obtained is significant when compared with the sampling distribution. This is not the only way of testing the Poisson hypothesis, and we shall meet another approach in the next chapter. We shall not go on to develop this method here but suppose that a significant result has been obtained for which an explanation is required.

One obvious direction to take is suggested by our discussion of mixtures in Chapter 2 and, especially, the idea of contributions to variation in Chapter 5. For definiteness we shall suppose that the original distribution referred to variation in the number of accidents. If the distributions of two or more groups are mixed, the variance of the mixture will be greater than the variances of either taken separately. This is because the combined variation has the 'between-groups variation' added to the 'within-group' variation attributable to the individual distributions. This might lead us to suspect that our single observed distribution was made up from groups having different accident rates. Thus if the data concerned the accident rates of bus drivers, it might be that drivers from different depots or different age groups had different accident rates. Guided by such speculations, we could examine each group individually to see whether they exhibited the Poisson form. As a result of such analyses we might arrive at fairly homogeneous subgroups which exhibited the 'Poisson' behaviour typical of a constant risk.

Unfortunately such a result would not be conclusive, because mixing is not the only way in which 'overdispersion' might occur. An alternative explanation might be found in what is sometimes called 'contagion'. It could be that having one accident would make it more, or less, likely that a driver would have further accidents. If this were so it would be impossible to distinguish between these hypotheses using the frequency distribution of the number of accidents alone. We do not intend to pursue this line of thinking further, but have included this discussion partly as an indication that statistical ideas can involve considerable subtlety which is easily passed over in more routine treatments.

Durations

In what we have done so far there was nothing special about the order in which the binary variables became available. Sometimes the ordering is significant and, if so, there may be characteristics of the binary sequence in which we might be interested. For example, how long we have to wait for the first 0. Such a waiting time is what we are now calling a *duration*. This sort of problem is most likely to arise when dealing with relatively rare events and it is in that context that we shall deal with it.

The simplest case is the waiting time for the first 1. The sum of two such intervals is the waiting time for the occurrence of the second 1; the sum of three is the waiting time for the third and so on. In Figure 11.3 we have supposed that the proportion of 1s in the population is 10% and we have then shown the distributions for 1, 2, 5 and 20 intervals.

The waiting time to the first occurrence has the *geometric* distribution with an average duration of 9. The subsequent distributions have averages which are 9 multiplied by the number of intervals. We notice that the form of the distribution appears to be tending to the Normal as the number of intervals in the sum increases. This behaviour is strongly reminiscent of the results we found by adding up exponentially distributed variables in Chapter 3 (see especially Figures 3.4 and 3.5). This similarity is no accident because the geometric and exponential distributions are very closely related, though we do not have the technical apparatus to pursue the connection here. However, this is a further example of the way that adding up independent variables tends to induce a degree of Normality. The distributions illustrated in Figure 11.3 are known as *negative binomial* distributions.

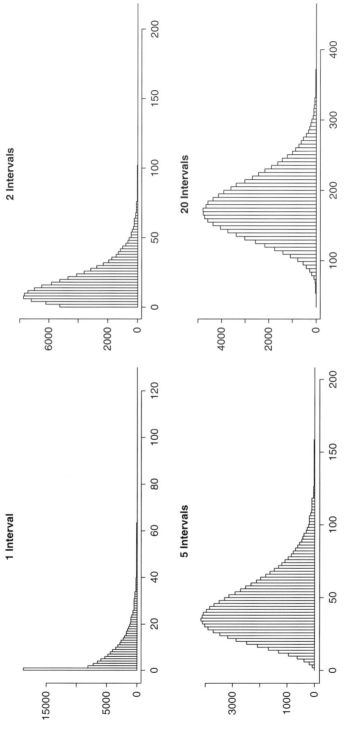

Figure 11.3 The distributions of waiting time for the occurrence of a 1 in a sequence of binary data

Relationship between Binary Variables

We noted earlier that if we assigned the codes 0 and 1 to the two outcomes of a binary variable we could treat those numbers as quantitative and compute such things as averages and variances from them. We can do the same sort of thing when we come to investigate relationships. We shall restrict the discussion to the case of two variables when the raw data might appear as follows:

(1,1), (0,1), (1,1), (0,0), (0,1), (1,1), …

In principle we could treat the 0s and 1s just like any other pairs of numbers and find, for example, their correlation coefficient. The point of treating them differently is that interesting connections with other methods emerge. We could begin by plotting a scatter diagram as in Figures 6.1 and 6.2, but a moment's thought will show that there is very little to be gained by doing this because all of the points would then be clustered together at the corners of a square. A more useful starting point is to construct a table showing how many pairs of each kind there are, as in Table 11.1. For obvious reasons this is sometimes called a *two by two table*.

Table 11.1   Two by two table

			Totals
	Number of (1,1) pairs	Number of (1,0) pairs	Number of 1s for first variable
	Number of (0,1) pairs	Number of (0,0) pairs	Number of 0s for first variable
Totals	Number of 1s for second variable	Number of 0s for second variable	Total frequency

From now on, for ease of reference, we shall call the first variable *A* and the second *B*. A typical table constructed on these lines might appear as in Table 11.2, where convenient round numbers have been selected to make it easier to see what is going on.

Table 11.2 Example of a table showing
the relationship between two binary
variables

		B		
		1	0	Total
A	1	35	11	46
	0	15	39	54
	Total	50	50	100

The binary variables 0 and 1 have been inserted into the blank row and column cells and the labels *A* and *B* denote the two variables. The total sample size is 100, of which there are 46 ones and 54 zeros for variable *A* and 50 of each for variable *B*. We are primarily interested in what the body of the table has to say about the relationship between the two variables. If there was a perfect relationship all pairs would be, as far as possible, in one of the cells (1,1) or (0,0). In other words, all the frequency would be concentrated on the diagonal cells. On the other hand, if there was no relationship at all, the columns, and rows, would be in the same proportion as the column, or row, totals. Measuring the strength of the relationship is therefore a matter of determining where the observed table lies between these two extremes.

We start by adopting a *regression* perspective, which means that we are interested in predicting one variable when we are given the other. Suppose that we know the value of variable *B* and wish to predict variable *A*. The obvious way to do this is to base the prediction in the relevant column of the table. Thus if the variable *B* is 1 the table tells us that a proportion 35/50 are 1s on variable *A*, whereas if *B* is 0 the proportion is only 11/50. This suggests that, if *A* is 1, there is a much greater chance of variable *B* also being 1. To place this confidence on a firmer footing we might test the significance of the difference between 35/50 and 11/50. This would be done by referring the difference to the sampling distribution of the difference of the two proportions. Bearing in mind that a proportion is also an average of the binary variables, it will have an approximately Normal sampling distribution. Further, since the difference between two Normal variables is also Normal, we have all the elements necessary for the test of significance and hence for constructing a confidence interval for the magnitude of the difference, if we so wish.

If we were to look at the problem from a *correlation* perspective, we would need a measure of the strength of any relationship. Correlation coefficients can be calculated for binary data in exactly the same way as for any other data, and all the cautions about correlation not implying causation set out in Chapter 6 apply here also. However, it is instructive to look at the problem in a slightly different way which anticipates the developments of the next chapter. We start with the table of frequencies as illustrated for the example in Table 11.2. It is easily possible to compute what frequencies we would have expected in that table if there were no correlation. We have already remarked that if there were no correlation the frequencies in the body of the table would be in the same proportions as in the margins. Thus because one half (50/100) of the total frequency were 1s on variable *B* we would expect the same to be true whatever the value of *A*.

Table 11.3   A table having the same marginal frequencies as Table 11.2 but showing what the cell frequencies would be if there were no correlation

		B		
		1	0	Total
A	1	23	23	46
	0	27	27	54
	Total	50	50	100

According to this reasoning the table of frequencies we would have expected if there were no correlation would be as in Table 11.3. All of the differences between the observed and these 'expected' frequencies, regardless of sign, are 12, and this is a measure of the degree of correlation, though it needs to be appropriately scaled to turn it into a recognisable correlation coefficient. The analysis of correlation for binary variables can thus be expressed in terms of how far a set of frequencies in a 2 × 2 table departs from expectation. The importance of this observation is that the same idea can be used for variables where the values can be classified into more than two categories.

12

GOODNESS OF FIT

Summary

Goodness of fit requires the comparison of a set of observed frequencies with their expectation on some hypothesis. A suitable test statistic is defined and its sampling distribution determined empirically. It is shown how this distribution depends on the number of frequencies being compared. It also depends on the number of parameters which have to be estimated, and this result is illustrated for the fit of a Normal distribution.

Introduction

This somewhat unusual title is firmly established in Statistics as the name for the matter of whether or not a set of frequencies conforms to that predicted by some theory. We met one such example at the end of the previous chapter where we had predictions for the frequencies in a 2 × 2 table. However, the question has been implicit in many other problems we have encountered. For example, we have talked rather loosely about whether or not a particular frequency distribution conformed to some theoretical form, such as the Normal distribution. In effect we were asking whether or not the frequencies which we observed to fall into particular categories were sufficiently close to what we would have expected, if they had come from a specified distribution. Similar problems arise in many other contexts.

We begin with a problem which has already occurred, though not as the main subject of interest. It we take a set of numbers from a random number table or generate them on a computer, the question naturally arises as to whether they are genuinely random. If they are there should be approximately equal numbers occurring in intervals of equal length. This was the situation pictured in Figures 1.8 and 1.9, where we supposed that numbers had been drawn uniformly from the interval (0,99). The numbers there were not exactly uniform and we might have asked whether the departure from uniformity was sufficient to warrant rejecting the hypothesis that they were random. That is the question we shall answer next.

Figure 1.8 was constructed by supposing that 200 numbers were taken at random from a table of random numbers. With the benefit of the knowledge of sampling we have acquired, we can describe this as sampling integers at random from a uniform distribution on the interval (0,99). Suppose this exercise is repeated and that the frequencies occurring in successive intervals turn out to be as in Table 12.1.

Table 12.1 Frequency distribution of 200 random numbers

0–9	10–19	20–29	30–39	40–49	50–59	60–69	70–79	80–89	90–99
21	23	18	16	23	19	18	26	22	14

If the numbers were truly random, we would expect the sampled values to be uniformly distributed across the range. By this we do not mean that there will be exactly 20 in each category because we have sampled at random; it means that there will be some variation but it will be consistent with this assumption. The question we now address is whether the variation we have observed in the table is or is not consistent with this hypothesis. We start by calculating what frequencies we would expect in each category. In this case the answer is simple because with a sample size of 200 and 10 categories we would obviously expect about 20, as we noted above. So the question now is: are the deviations of the above frequencies sufficient to call into question the randomness of the numbers in the Table 12.1?

This question is rather more complicated than any we have met before. When considering the test for the difference between two averages, for example, the natural thing to do seemed to be to work with the difference between the sample averages. Here it is not quite so obvious what the test statistic should be. There are, in fact, many ways in which it can be done, and two of them are commonly used in practice. This is a point at which we may justly feel the need for some theoretical guidance which it is not possible to give with our self-imposed limitation of no mathematics. It is nevertheless possible, with a combination of intuition and results that we already have, to provide a plausible argument for one of the commonly used tests.

To begin with, it is clear that we need some way of measuring the discrepancy indicated by Table 12.1. If we had such a measure we could find its sampling distribution empirically and judge significance in the same way as with any other test. Such a measure obviously needs to depend on the differences between the actual frequencies and those we expect. The expected frequency is 20 in each case, and the differences in the above example are therefore: 1, 3, –2, –4, 3, –1, –2, 6, 2, –6. The most obvious measure is, perhaps, the sum of these differences, but that suggestion is immediately ruled out because the sum is zero. Furthermore, this will always be the case, because the observed and the expected frequencies always have the same sum. Taking our cue from earlier work on the variance, the next thought might be to add up the values regardless of sign or add up their squares. This is certainly possible but this, too, has drawbacks, as the following consideration shows. Suppose we consider one particular category for which the expected value is 2000 and for which the observed frequency is 2004. The difference is only 4, and intuition suggests that this is a much less serious deviation than if the expected value had been 10 and the observed frequency 14. The difference is 4 in each case, but a difference of 4 from 2000 seems much less serious than a difference of 4 from 10. This intuition may, of course, be unsound, but it should caution us against too readily adopting the first measure that comes to mind.

A better, though admittedly tenuous, line of reasoning is as follows. Let us focus on one category in particular and ask how we might measure the discrepancy in that case. This problem is rather similar to the problem of a test for a single proportion, because here we have an observed proportion to be compared with one predicted by theory. When setting up a test for that much simpler problem, we expressed the deviation as a multiple of the standard error. The standard error in this case is the binomial variance, which we know to be a little less than the average. If the probability were to be small enough we know that the relevant sampling distribution would have the Poisson form, for which the variance would be precisely equal to the average. If then we were to divide each departure from expectation by the square root of the expectation, which is the standard error, we would have the right sort of measure for that particular category. One possible way of getting an overall measure of discrepancy is then to add up the squares of these individual measures. This gives us what is one of the commonly used measures of *goodness of fit*. Once we have such a measure, we can determine its empirical sampling distribution and, from that, judge significance in the usual way. Performing this operation for the example of Table 12.1, we obtain the following value for our measure of goodness of fit:

1/20 + 9/20 + 4/20 + 16/20 + 9/20 + 1/20 + 4/20 + 36/20 + 4/20 + 36/20

This gives

0.050 + 0.450 + 0.200 + 0.800 + 0.45 + 0.050 + 0.200 + 1.800 + 0.200 + 1.800 = 6.000

This number measures the closeness of the observed set of frequencies to those expected under the hypothesis that the original values were taken from a table of random numbers. It is certainly greater than zero, indicating that the fit is not perfect, but whether or not it is too large for us to reasonably conclude that the numbers in the table are not truly random has yet to be determined. The whole calculation may be set out in a standard tabular form which is often used (see Table 12.2). The total of the last column is 6.000, which is the measure of goodness of fit.

Table 12.2 Calculation of the goodness-of-fit statistic for the example in Table 12.1

Variable interval	Observed frequency (O)	Expected frequency (E)	(O–E)	(O–E)²/E
0–9	21	20	1	0.050
10–19	23	20	3	0.450
20–29	18	20	–2	0.200
30–39	16	20	–4	0.800
40–49	23	20	3	0.450
50–59	19	20	–1	0.050
60–69	18	20	–2	0.200
70–79	26	20	6	1.800
80–89	22	20	2	0.200
90–99	14	20	–6	1.800

The Sampling Distribution

The value of 6.000 which we obtained as the measure of goodness of fit in the example above tells us little by itself. We need to know whether it is consistent with the hypothesis that the distribution was, in fact, uniform. To make this judgement we need the sampling distribution of the measure of goodness of fit. This can be obtained in the usual way by drawing random samples from the uniform distribution and calculating the measure of fit for each sample. The sampling distribution, based on 100,000 samples, shown in Figure 12.1 was obtained in this way.

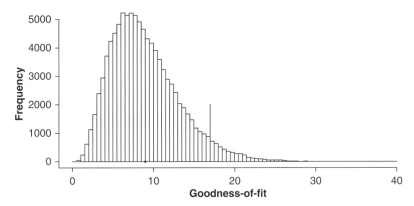

Figure 12.1 Sampling distribution of goodness-of-fit (GF) statistic showing the average (9) and upper 5% point (16.9)

The observed value is, in fact, less than the average so it is perfectly consistent with the hypothesis that the distribution was uniform. The result shows that we would not have grounds for questioning this conclusion unless the measure exceeded 17, say.

Unlike many sampling distributions which we have met so far, this sampling distribution is skewed, with its upper tail longer than its lower. More important is the fact that here we are only interested in the upper tail because it is only large values of the measure which count against the hypothesis. Very small values, in the lower tail, might arouse suspicions, but only on non-statistical grounds. A famous example of this occurred in the case of Gregor Mendel's experiments on breeding peas. To corroborate his hypothesis of inheritance it was necessary to obtain a set of frequencies consistent with the theory. It appears that the fit Mendel obtained was actually too good when judged by a goodness-of-fit test! However the situation was examined in great detail by Sir Ronald Fisher who concluded that all was well.

There are, however, other legitimate questions which may be raised about our analysis. The choice of the number of intervals into which we divided the range was arbitrary. What would have happened if we had used five intervals, or even 100? Obviously we would have obtained a different answer, but would the conclusion have been different? These are important questions which we shall not pursue here, but there is one rather obvious point to be made. If the intervals are very wide there is the possibility that there might be some departure from the hypothesis lying wholly within a single interval which we should miss altogether. This argues for more rather than fewer intervals.

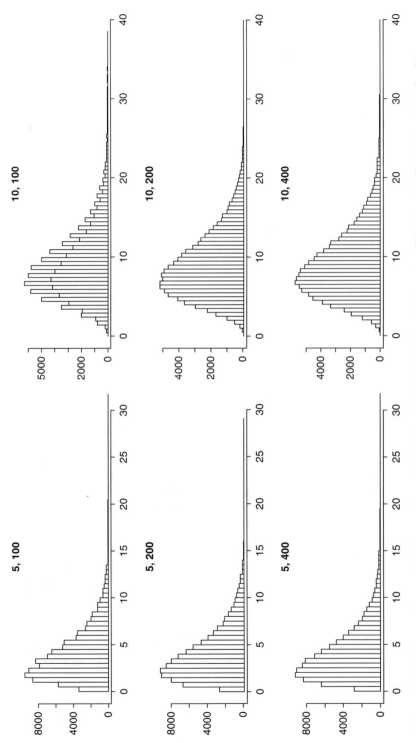

Figure 12.2 Dependence of the sampling distribution on the number of categories (first number) and the sample size (second number)

We also do not know whether the sampling distribution depends on the sample size. The effect of sample size and the number of intervals on the sampling distribution can easily be investigated empirically, and some illustrative results are shown in Figure 12.2.

Looking down the left- or right-hand side of Figure 12.2, we notice very little change in the distribution, so the sampling distribution appears not to depend too critically on the sample size. This is one consequence of the form of the measure we selected for goodness of fit. The rather sketchy argument we offered to justify that choice is not wholly sufficient to ensure that property, but it is reassuring to note that our calculations support it. Moving from left to right across Figure 12.2 we see that the distribution does depend on the number of categories. The average happens to be one less than the number of categories, and this result holds quite generally. The middle distribution on the right-hand side is equivalent to the one shown in Figure 12.1. There is one other noteworthy thing about these distributions. There is a somewhat jagged appearance to the outline of the histograms when the sample size is 100, and this gets 'smoothed' out as the sample size increases. This is because both the observed and expected frequencies have to be whole numbers.

For this reason, when calculating their contributions to the overall goodness of fit, only certain values can actually occur, so the histogram exhibits the resulting irregularities until the sample size is large enough to render them negligible.

Goodness of Fit of a Normal Distribution

Testing the goodness of fit for a Normal distribution raises some new, and subtle, features which did not occur with the uniform distribution, but we first deal with a very simple extension of the fit of a uniform distribution. In the latter case the distribution we were fitting was completely defined by the fact that it was uniform with range 0–99. To illustrate the position with a completely defined Normal distribution, we shall take the data already used in Figure 3.6 for which the sample size was exactly 100. At that stage we had not met the phenomenon of sampling and the data were treated at a purely descriptive level. The data were, in fact, obtained as a random sample from a Normal population with average zero and standard deviation 100. To test the hypothesis that the sample is consistent with having been sampled, as we have claimed, from such a Normal distribution we first have to calculate how many values should occur in successive intervals. We are free to specify the number and width of these intervals, and then we calculate the measure of goodness of fit as before. To keep things as simple as possible, a small number of intervals has been chosen. The calculations have been set out in Table 12.3 in the standard format.

Table 12.3 Calculation of the goodness of fit for a Normal distribution

Interval	O	E	(O–E)	(O–E)²/E
Less than –125	10	10.56	–0.56	0.030
–125 to –75	14	12.10	1.90	0.298
–75 to –25	20	17.47	–2.53	0.366
–25 to 0	10	9.87	0.13	0.002
0 to 25	6	9.87	–3.87	1.517
25–125	19	17.47	1.53	0.134
75 to 125	8	12.10	–4.10	0.389
more than 125	13	10.56	2.44	0.564
Total	100	100.00		4.298

The intervals were chosen to give moderate expected frequencies. There is some evidence that one should try to make the expected frequencies roughly equal, and our choice has been made with that recommendation in mind, but this is something which need not trouble us too much here. If we calculate the same measure of goodness of fit as we used for the uniform distribution in Table 12.3, we obtain the value of 4.298. To judge the significance of this value we must obtain the empirical sampling distribution of the goodness-of-fit statistic and this has been shown in Figure 12.3.

This is essentially the same sort of distribution as that given in Figure 12.1, but the average there was 9 instead of 7 obtained for this distribution. In fact the form does not depend on what distribution we are fitting, and all that matters is the frequencies falling into the various intervals. The observed value (4.298) is again less than the average of the sampling distribution, and so there is no question of the deviation being significant.

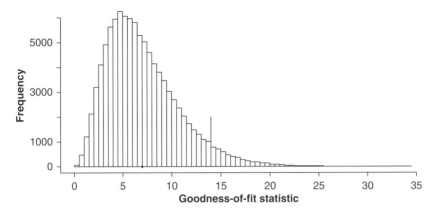

Figure 12.3 Approximate sampling distribution of goodness-of-fit statistic for a known Normal distribution showing the average value of 7

We conclude this section by mentioning another goodness-of-fit problem. Its full solution would take us beyond the limits of this book, but we mention it to give a glimpse beyond the boundary we have set ourselves. This will serve to show that the basic ideas of inference which have served us hitherto need some elaboration.

Suppose we were given the same sample of data as in the last example based on the Normal distribution and were asked to test whether it could have been sampled at random from *any* Normal distribution whatsoever, that is, one with the average and variance unspecified. The usual, and natural, first step is to use the average and variance of the sample being tested as a substitute for the true, but unknown, values. This enables us to calculate expected frequencies, and to compute the goodness-of-fit statistic in the usual way. The trouble comes at the next step where the earlier procedure would require us to compute the sampling distribution by drawing repeated random samples in the same manner as the one already to hand. But we do not know what population it has come from because the hypothesis we are trying to test does not specify the average and variance of that population. How, then, can we possibly make a test of significance? It is tempting to compute the goodness-of-fit statistic in the usual way, but that would be wrong because it makes no allowance for the fact that we are constrained by the sampling distribution, which will have to be such that every sample considered will have the same average and variance as the sample under test. What we really need, therefore, is a constrained sampling distribution allowing for that requirement. It is easy to obtain that distribution theoretically, and students are taught that the degrees of freedom (the same as the average here) of the sampling distribution must be reduced by 2 – one for the average and one for the variance. To confirm this empirically we would have to produce the sampling distribution incorporating these constraints. If we had done this the sampling distribution would turn out to be as shown in Figure 12.4, where the average of the distribution is 5 as we predicted.

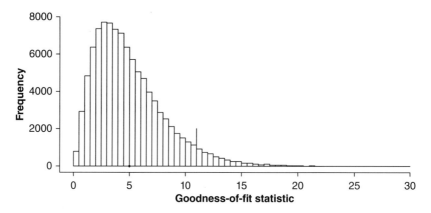

Figure 12.4 Sampling distribution of goodness-of-fit statistic for the estimated Normal distribution

The 2 x 2 Table

For our final example we return to the data given in the final section of the previous chapter. There we were discussing the correlation of binary variables, but there is an obvious similarity with the idea of goodness of fit which we shall now employ. In Table 11.3 we gave the frequencies we would expect if there were no relationship. Evidence of a correlation was to be found by looking to see how far the actual frequency was from that expected. There is one striking feature of Figure 12.5 on which we have not commented on before. The distribution is discrete in the sense that the goodness-of-fit statistic only takes particular values. This is not surprising when we remember that the statistic is a very simple quantity which is calculated from whole numbers. This is a common feature when dealing with goodness of fit and it means that we have to modify slightly the way in which we carry out a significance test. In the case of the present example we discover from the sampling distribution that the chance that the test statistic is at most 4 is 0.070 and that it is at least 5 is 0.026. There is therefore no precise 5% significance level. A value of about 4 would make us doubtful about the hypothesis, whereas a modest increase to 5 would make the result much more conclusive.

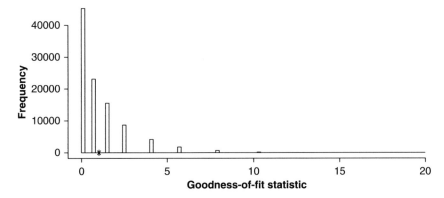

Figure 12.5 Sampling distribution of goodness-of-fit statistic for Table 11.3

13

UNOBSERVED VARIABLES

Summary

Unobserved variables can sometimes be studied through other variables with which they are correlated. Such variables may be pure constructs, which cannot be observed, even in principle. Intelligence is one such variable, and this is used in this chapter to illustrate the problems of measurement and interpretation which arise. The relevance of earlier parts of the book in relation to these problems is demonstrated, especially that relating to the 'nature versus nurture' debate.

Introduction

It may seem paradoxical that one should attempt to study unobserved variables, but this is often possible through their relationship with variables which can be observed. Unobserved variables are important in the social sciences. Variables may be unobserved because they have been lost, or simply missed, and this often happens in surveys. However, here we shall be interested in variables which are unobserved for more fundamental reasons. For example, it may be that they cannot be observed because they concern some sensitive subject on which direct questions cannot be put in a survey. Here, however, we shall go one step further and be concerned with variables which are unobservable in principle. Our attention will be focused on one such variable, namely human intelligence, which is both very important and often highly controversial. There are many other such variables relating to attitudes and opinions, and much of what we have to say will be relevant to them also, but by keeping the spotlight on one particular variable some of the main problems will become apparent.

Intelligence does not exist in the sense that one cannot make any physical measurement on the brain which has undisputed claims to be regarded as intelligence. Yet some people undoubtedly behave as if intelligence were an attribute of the human person which can be possessed in varying degrees. They speak of it in the same terms as any other physical quantity which can be measured. Is there any rational basis for such behaviour which would allow it to be treated by the methods available for all the other variables covered in this book?

The discussion of such matters is not helped by the fact that a great variety of names exist to describe such variables which owe more to their disciplinary origins and the somewhat blinkered viewpoint of their proponents than to their essential character. The adjectives *latent* and *hidden* are both accurate and descriptive, but few would guess, without prompting, that a *factor*, in this context, is the same as a latent variable.

This topic is included in the book because it is important for social scientists to know something about it and it enables us to illustrate some of the elementary ideas expounded earlier in the book. From the historical point of view, there have been two apparently different approaches to the subject whose common purpose is not always recognised. We shall take each in turn and show how they are, in reality, two different approaches to the same end.

The 'Spurious Correlation' Approach

In Chapter 6 we introduced the idea of spurious correlation, and there our remarks were intended to serve as a warning that if two variables were correlated that did not mean that they were causally linked. Here we turn that phenomenon to advantage by developing the idea that correlation can also be indicative of a common dependence on a third variable. The basis of our contention is that an apparent correlation between two variables can be 'induced' by their common dependence on another variable. More generally, if a collection of observable variables are mutually correlated this may be because they are all causally linked to some unobserved variable. In other words, the existence of a number, preferably a large number, of mutually correlated variables is a pointer to the possible existence of an underlying unobserved variable which may be of much greater interest. This was recognised by Charles Spearman in a study published in 1904. He noted that children who performed well in one kind of school test tended to perform well in other tests of a similar kind. This observation led him to postulate that there was a common underlying ability, possessed by children, which reflected their general ability. Spearman wished to avoid the connotations which might be attached to the concept if he called it 'intelligence' so he used the more neutral symbol g. Spearman's g-factor thus entered the world of intelligence testing where it has remained ever since. What he had showed, first of all, was that the observed correlations could be explained by the existence of an unobserved quantity which he called g. He had not shown that this *had* to be the explanation. In fact Godfrey Thomson showed that exactly the same pattern of correlations could be explained by what subsequently came to be called his 'bonds model'. Although the debate about it between the two continued for 30 years, Spearman never seems to have been persuaded. To make his discovery useful, Spearman had to go on to show how to calculate where a person lay on the g-scale. He did this using what subsequently came to be recognised as the first example of factor analysis. However, the crucial first step was to realise that the discovery of a number of mutually correlated variables could be indicative of an underlying variable which might be of great practical importance. Spurious correlation is always a possibility when looking at the correlations between variables, but it may be the prelude to defining an unobservable or 'latent' variable which generates the correlations.

The Index Approach

A quite different line of approach was pioneered by Binet and Terman, whose names are particularly associated with the early construction and use of IQ tests. Their approach has become the dominant approach in intelligence testing and, incidentally, has also attracted most of the criticism. We call this the index approach, using the term 'index' to refer to any quantity which we calculate from a set of data. An average is thus an index in this sense because it is computed from any set of numbers. In the present context the intelligence quotient (IQ) is an index since it is calculated from a set of scores obtained by subjects performing 'paper and pencil' tests. To many people intelligence testing is equated with IQ and many have a general idea of what it means to have an IQ of 95 or 120, for example.

One should not be distracted by the fact that intelligence testing was first applied, by Binet, to children because of the desire to identify the need for additional education. Although this fact has influenced the terminology, especially the word 'quotient', the idea has now been adopted much more widely. However, the term IQ is now so firmly attached to the word 'intelligence' in the context of intelligence testing as to make them inseparable.

The essential idea of the index approach is to select a set of 'tests' which are then given to subjects. Their answers are scored and the scores are added up to give a measure of intelligence. There are many variations and refinements of this procedure, but this simple specification captures the essentials. Constructing a test involves starting from some notion of what intelligence is, then constructing test items which span the range of what one believes intelligence to be, before administering the test to samples of the population to which one wishes to apply the results. Elementary statistical ideas are called into play in implementing this procedure.

The result of testing will be a frequency distribution of total test scores. In practice the form of this is often close to the Normal distribution. One might have expected this because the total score is obtained by adding up the scores on individual items. However, as we shall see, the conditions required by the central limit theorem, which we met briefly in Chapter 3, will not necessarily be met. The principal remaining statistical problem is one of calibration which is needed if we wish to make an objective statement about where one individual stands on the scale in relation to another. This is where the results about shifting distributions and rescaling them, discussed in Chapter 2, are called into play. In practice this is done by arranging for the average of the distribution to be 100. It could equally have been zero or 10,000, but long-standing convention dictates that it should be 100. We therefore calibrate the distribution by shifting it so that its average is 100. An intelligence measure is therefore immediately known to be above or below the population average by whether or not it is above or below 100. It is also convenient to measure deviations from the average in units of the standard deviation which, by convention, is taken to be 15. Thus, for example, a person whose intelligence score is one standard deviation above the average is given a score of 115. If the distribution were precisely Normal, we could immediately translate this into the proportion of the population with a score greater than 115 – and so on.

The meaning and validity of this method depend very heavily on the selection of test items, and it is this feature which has attracted most of the criticism. It is alleged, for example, that such tests are culturally biased because those who select the test items will, unconsciously or otherwise, select items which are more favourable to those who share their cultural background. This aspect has been particularly prominent in the long-running dispute about the relative intelligence of black and white subjects. The method is inevitably subjective because the set of test items has to be constructed by people similar to those who apply the tests. It may appear that statistical ideas only play a secondary role and that is only after the items have been selected. We shall explore the nature of this claim in more detail.

The set of possible test items is called the 'domain' – not the 'population', which would be the natural term for a statistician. The domain is usually very poorly defined because the items are constructed – not selected – and there is no obvious limit to the number of elements which belong to the domain. The considerable success of intelligence testing in practice has been largely due to the success of practitioners in producing sets of items which have commanded a large measure of agreement. The position can be set out schematically in a way which may help to make the position clearer.

A typical set of data may appear as follows:

		PERSONS							
		1	2	3	4	5	6	7	...
TESTS	1								
	2								
	3								
	4								
	...								

The numbers in each cell of the table are the scores for each individual on each particular test. If the 'persons' have been selected randomly from some population then the methods of inference given in the latter half of this book can be used to make statements about the population from which they have been drawn. For example, each person will have a total score whose distribution, average, or any such summary, can be used to make inferences about the corresponding population characteristics. However, the test items are clearly not a random sample from any population whatsoever. Indeed, the population is not well defined. In particular, we should infer that the total score is approximately

Normal simply because it is a total. Adding up is not, of itself, sufficient to produce Normality – we also need the randomness of the sampling method, which is lacking here. This fact causes much confusion because it often happens that such distributions are close to the Normal form. It is this fact which has given rise to the term 'bell curve' to describe the shape of the distribution. It is undoubtedly true that test designers seek to make their selections representative in some sense, but it is not the representativeness of random sampling which would automatically produce Normality.

To summarise: the index method leading to IQ is a natural and read-ily comprehended measure of intelligence. It is essentially a total, suitably calibrated, of test scores. The great weakness of the approach is that its value depends on the domain from which the test items are selected, and this, at bottom, is a subjective matter. It is the domain which embodies what the test constructor(s) understand by the word 'intelligence' and in so far as this is accepted as appropriate, IQ will be deemed a satisfactory measure. There is, however, no ultimate defence against the criticism that the domain simply reflects the prejudices or unrecognised biases of the constructors.

There is a more subtle criticism of IQ which does not derive from the subjectivity of the domain. This is that intelligence is not a one-dimensional entity which can be measured on a single scale. This criticism is often expressed by saying that human intelligence is a many-sided thing. It has even given rise to other kinds of intelligence such as *emotional intelligence*. It is argued that cognitive ability takes many forms not all of which can be captured by numbers on a single dimension. The idea is familiar enough in other spheres. For example, athletic ability varies a great deal but exists in many forms. There are track and field events which call for different skills or physiques. Any attempt to construct a single measure of athletic ability would be laughed out of court on these grounds alone. When national prestige is measured by the number of medals won, there is an immediate outcry when it is proposed to add or remove particular sports. For to do so would indirectly affect the standing of nations with particular strengths or weaknesses in the fields which were being targeted. This is exactly analogous to the criticism that cultural bias is introduced into IQ meas-ures by the definition of the domain.

The 'spurious correlation' approach is capable of handling the 'many dimensions' problem, but to pursue this would take us into deeper water than this book has prepared us for. We shall therefore conclude this chap-ter by only going far enough to acquaint ourselves with some of the new problems which arise; in particular, some of the consequences of allowing latent variables to be two-dimensional. This takes us back to Chapter 6 on covariation.

One of the problems with the index approach is that it prejudges the question of whether or not intelligence is a quantity varying along a single dimension. An advantage of the 'spurious correlation' approach is that it leaves this question open. However, although we shall not be able to go into this in any depth, we can make a very elementary point which is often overlooked. This is that, once more than one dimension is allowed for, there is no longer any guarantee of our being able to order or rank individuals according to their intelligence. The point at issue is illustrated in Figure 13.1. When interpreting this it may be helpful to think of the analogy with the location of places on a map. We need two dimensions for this, and hence maps are two-dimensional objects which we use to find our way. Similarly, if there are just two kinds of intelligence which, purely for illustration, we might call verbal and numerical intelligence, we need two dimensions to describe the position of an individual. If intelligence were only one-dimensional, then it would be possible to place individuals along a line where position represents *intelligence*; IQ is such an example. If one dimension is not adequate we might be in one of the positions shown in Figure 13.1 when comparing two individuals, denoted there by A and B. If things are as in the top diagram, there is no problem about ranking A and B. Whether we use the vertical or the horizontal dimensions, A comes out on top because his score is higher than B's whichever type of intelligence we choose to use. In the second diagram the position is reversed because A is better in the horizontal direction but poorer in the vertical direction. This shows that we cannot necessarily rank the two individuals using only a pair of measures. Finally, we come to the third diagram, which is much less clear-cut and rather similar to what we find in the real world.

In one sense this tells the same story as the middle diagram of Figure 13.1, which ranks B higher on the vertical dimension but lower on the horizontal dimension. However, one's eye is drawn to the dashed line which represents the major direction of variation, and this would give A the advantage. We might sensibly decide to use the horizontal dimension which is clearly dominant.

This explains why it may be sensible to allow that intelligence may actually be many-dimensional and, at the same time, to use a dominant dimension and designate it by some term such as 'general intelligence' since it will serve tolerably well most of the practical purposes for which such measures are required.

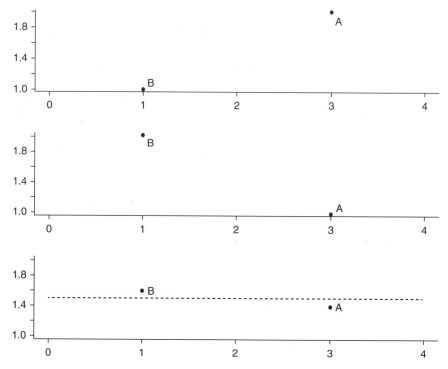

Figure 13.1 Some possible orderings of individuals A and B in two dimensions

The Inheritance of Intelligence: Nature versus Nurture

The basic ideas of Statistics are very useful when evaluating the arguments about the extent to which intelligence is inherited. It is commonly assumed that individual characteristics are partly determined by what is inherited from parents, through the genes, and partly by the environment. This is what is known as the *nature versus nurture* issue. Such arguments usually centre on a measure of inheritance which is expressed as a proportion or a percentage. Thus it may be claimed, for example, that 50% of intelligence is inherited.

The measure of heritability used goes back to Sir Ronald Fisher, who proposed it in connection with inheritance among plants and animals, though it has achieved prominence through its use on human populations. Unsurprisingly, in view of Fisher's association with the analysis of variance, it depends on much the same ideas as the analysis of variation discussed in Chapter 5. In a population any chosen characteristic will vary and, in part, this variation can be attributed to either parentage or the environment. Taking our cue from our earlier work on variation, we may therefore try to decompose that variation into its two constituent parts. If this is possible, a measure of inheritance may be constructed by comparing the two parts. More precisely, the proportion of variation attributable to intelligence can be used as the measure of heritability. Even from this sketchy definition, one fact is very obvious, which is often overlooked. The measure proposed is a characteristic of the population and not of the individual. This means that it is only sensible to compare populations which are otherwise similar, or to make comparisons within the same population over time if nothing else has changed. For example, suppose that 50% of the variation in a specified population is due to environmental factors. The discovery of this fact might be followed by educational reform whose intended effect was to reduce the effects of educational disadvantage. If this reform was effective it would reduce the environmental component of variation and therefore increase the proportion of variation due to inheritance. This would produce the apparent paradox that heritability had increased whereas, in reality, there had been no change whatsoever in the real role of the genes.

In reality things are more complex than the construction of this simple measure suggests. For example, there might be an interaction between the environment and the mechanism of inheritance, which means that the effect of environmental factors might be changed depending on what happened to the strength of heritability. There should, however, be no difficulty in measuring the total variation if we can obtain a random sample from the relevant population. If we can measure the total variation, we need to be able to measure either the environmental or genetic variation, or both. We have taken this for granted; it can be done, but it is a non-trivial matter.

Latent Variables in Social Science

Intelligence is only one example of an unobservable variable of interest to social scientists, and in many ways it is not typical. Such measures may relate to individuals or groups and include a whole range of attitudes and abilities. Educational opportunity and political conservatism are examples which can relate to either individuals or groups. Researchers are usually interested in the relationships between such variables, and especially the causal links which may connect them. We have had a little to say about relationships, mainly in Chapter 6, but only in the context of observable variables. In order to elucidate the relationships between latent variables, one possibility is to construct indices to represent such variables and then to investigate the relationship between them by traditional methods. A second possibility is to infer the relationships between the latent variables from the observable relationships between the observable variables. In practice the information required is contained in the covariances. Hence the technique is often referred to as *covariance structure analysis*. This is a popular approach but it is beset by hazards, not the least of which is that there may be more than one situation in the latent world which leads to identical consequences for what can be observed in the observable world. The ramifications of this remark lie far beyond the bounds of the present book.

14

RETROSPECT

Summary

This chapter reviews the topics covered in the book and sets them in the wider context of the field of Statistics and its place as part of scientific method. It concludes with a brief review of other relevant literature.

Review

This chapter may be read from at least two perspectives. The first is that of beginners who have read this far and should, by now, have some idea of what Statistics is all about. For them this chapter is to smooth the path to more traditional texts which emphasise methods. The second perspective is that of teachers who have looked at the subject again through the lens offered by this book and wish to relate it to what they have been teaching hitherto.

After the absence of mathematics, the most obvious feature of the book is, perhaps, the much greater amount of space given to descriptive methods. In one sense this is a direct result of the decision to make the frequency distribution the key element of the exposition. Until the student has a good grasp of how variation occurs and what happens when it is manipulated, the subtler points of the subject will never be clear. However, from a more fundamental standpoint, an important aim of the book is to expose the basic rationale which lies beneath much routine statistical activity. This is most clearly demonstrated, perhaps, by the analysis of variation first treated in Chapter 5. Students first meet this usually in the context of hypothesis testing and easily miss the basic idea which gives rise to it. It is fundamentally about identifying sources of variation, and the idea behind this can be most simply explained in descriptive terms, as in Chapter 5. Testing whether any decomposition arrived at is 'significant' is, strictly speaking, a secondary, though important, matter which is best postponed until the reason for looking at the problem in the first place has become clearer.

As we noted at the beginning, although it is true that most elementary texts begin with frequency distributions, they rapidly move on in their haste to reach inferential procedures, which leads many people to suppose that is what the subject is really about. Here we have not only spent time on the many kinds of variation which arise in practice but also given introductory descriptive accounts of topics such as regression analysis, as well as the analysis of variation. The reader should expect to gain a better understanding of these relatively advanced techniques before becoming involved with the details of testing.

The same point can be put in a rather more sophisticated way by saying that the emphasis may be said to have shifted from parameters to the distributions which they purport to describe. This shows itself rather subtly in Chapter 6 where we refer to tests being concerned with whether two Normal distributions having the same variance are the same rather than whether two normal distributions have the same average. These are equivalent statements, but the first makes the form of the distribution central instead of its average. This is partly why there is nothing at all in the book about the median, mode, geometric mean or any other measure of location, as they are collectively described. This is not because they are unimportant, but because this is a book about ideas, and the idea in this case is sufficiently contained in the average which alone has been used here. Indeed, this restriction has led to a terminological problem about what to call it. Many measures of location are often called 'means'. This covers a family which includes the arithmetic, harmonic and geometric means. This matter is made doubly confusing because all of these means are sometimes also known as averages! We have preferred the word 'average' throughout because it is the most rudimentary, and is widely understood: it is the total divided by the number of cases.

A similar point arises with measures of dispersion. There are many but we have used just one – the standard deviation. This is not the simplest to calculate, and beginners often think it is unnecessarily complicated. But when we come to realise that the analysis of variance, which embodies some of the most fundamental ideas of Statistics, cannot do without it, the effort seems worthwhile.

No two elementary texts on Statistics cover the same ground. Our treatment probably goes beyond what would normally be covered in a first-year course for social scientists. This is partly because so many topics which are covered in those courses have been deliberately omitted. This, of course, is the result of our concentration on ideas rather than methods. However, this very fact has made it clear just how far the basic ideas of the subject can take us into territory which would normally be closed to beginners. I hope that this fact alone will help to create the impression that Statistics is not such a difficult subject after all – even if it is challenging!

The computer has brought about two major revolutions in Statistics. The first, which has often been noticed, is that computers are very fast and accurate calculating machines. This has removed much of the drudgery of traditional Statistics, especially at the elementary level. There are, however, good grounds for arguing that students should carry out the standard calculations at least once in their lives because of the insight which they give into the ideas to which the calculations give expression. In the present book almost all the calculation lies beneath the surface. A few explicit calculations are given only where they would help to make clear what is going on.

The second revolution is more fundamental and not so readily recognised. Statistical tables, which students had to use and often own, are now obsolete – in principle at least. No use has been made of them in this book. More fundamentally, we can also almost dispense with probability theory which has been held to be necessary to understand inferential procedures. This is because all of the sampling distributions required can be generated empirically by actual sampling as and when needed – as they have been in this book, although the details may not always be obvious. What is more, we can generate new distributions to solve problems which would have been beyond reach at an elementary level until quite recently. All of this depends on the existence of random number generators in computers. Furthermore, the whole business can be done very rapidly on an ordinary laptop computer. In this book sampling distributions have been generated from 100,000 random samples (quite enough to give adequate precision) in a matter of seconds – rarely longer. This is less time than it would take to look them up in a book or find the relevant table in a set of statistical tables.

Statistical inference requires us to compare what has actually happened with what might have happened. This is done via the sampling distribution. The approach to significance tests in this book has a rather different emphasis than that found in most elementary texts, especially those written for social scientists. Such texts often make it appear that testing significance is the be-all and end-all of Statistics. In fact, some go so far as to provide tabular layouts designed to help students find their way through the jungle of tests on offer. Here we have used a rather more informal and parsimonious approach. Although it is not unusual to find the experts in any field adopting an apparently less rigorous approach to procedures than is taught to beginners, I have tried not to go too far in that direction.

The tendency among social scientists at large, especially those who are untutored in statistical matters, is to attribute 'significance' to almost any observed difference. The great practical value of significance tests is in their negative role in putting a brake on such tendencies. The chief, negative, lesson of significance testing is in showing that it is important to know what variation is likely to be encountered in the absence of real effects. For this reason we have laid emphasis on the whole sampling distribution rather than a few arbitrary significance levels. In addition to the distribution itself, we have usually given the average of the distribution. This gives an idea of what variation is to be expected even if the hypothesis being tested is true. When the sampling distribution is close to Normal, its average and its standard error almost tell the whole story. When we know these two numbers we can immediately use the limits, which we recommended memorising in Chapter 4 (see Figure 4.1), to delineate the sampling variation which is to be expected from that which is not. When the sampling distribution is skewed and we are only interested in the upper tail the average, supplemented by the upper 5% point or some similar critical point, gives a rough idea of how large the test statistic needs to be before one begins to suspect that the hypothesis is false. Other percentage points can, of course, be used and one must not give the impression that such levels may be chosen arbitrarily to suit one's own preconceived opinions! The ubiquitous P-values of 0.05 or 0.01 are not to be despised. Here we are simply signalling a change of emphasis which needs to be made as a counterweight to much current practice.

Another important feature of our treatment is that the ideas behind statistical inference are approached in easy stages. The first step is to introduce the idea of sampling as we have done in Chapter 7. Only then do we move on to introduce the first main idea of inference by limiting the discussion to the case of a single observation. This may not be recognisably 'inference' at all, as in practice we usually have a sample, not a single observation. Nevertheless, this approach provides a natural introduction to the central idea of the sampling distribution of a statistic, which is the main subject of Chapter 9. Only then are we ready to begin a discussion of the basic tests of significance which occupy

Chapters 10 and 11, though Chapters 12 and 13 also provide a good deal on testing significance.

One advantage of our empirical approach is that it is very easy to bring the idea of the power of a test into the picture. Power can be estimated as a proportion in exactly the same way as a significance level. It can thus be easily computed in a routine fashion, especially in cases where a theoretical investigation would be prohibitively difficult.

In this book we have covered both tests of hypotheses and interval estimation, though the former have received the greater emphasis. We have given a brief treatment of interval estimation mainly in Chapter 8, but this concerns only a single average. Interval estimation is concerned with the interval within which something like an unknown average may be expected to lie. The emphasis on hypothesis testing is contrary to the advice of some statisticians, and it is instructive to consider the reason for this difference. The reason is simple. Interval estimation usually requires a fuller specification of the distributions under consideration, and this is often not available at an elementary level – especially in the social sciences. Most interval estimation is concerned with the values of *parameters* which occur in the specification of statistical models. A parameter is anything like the average or variance of a population which tells us about some aspect of a distribution such as its location or shape. Only when we have a fairly detailed knowledge of what is going on are parameters likely to be meaningful. Prior to that, we are more often in the position of needing to answer less specific questions about distributions which can often only be handled by testing hypotheses.

The reader may have heard of Bayesian methods and wonder why there is no mention of them in this book. The answer is simple. Bayes' theorem, on which that whole approach depends, is a theorem in mathematics – the mathematics of probability – and any treatment of statistics using Bayesian methods is necessarily mathematical. In practice the two approaches often lead to identical or very similar results, even if the interpretation is subtly different. However, if a totally non-mathematical treatment is required, Bayesian methods are not an option. Nevertheless, it is worth mentioning that there is no essential difference between the idea of a frequency distribution of a variable, on which our treatment is based, and the probability distribution which is the starting point of Bayesian methods. Indeed, Bayesian methods start by quantifying uncertainty, and uncertainty is the complementary idea to variation which we have made our starting point. If something is varying it is uncertain what the next value will be!

As we have repeatedly emphasised, variation may arise in one of two ways. The first, with which Chapters 1–6 were concerned, is that which occurs naturally in the phenomena we study. The second, which arises in inference, is the variation which *might* have occurred had we drawn repeated random samples instead of having only the one to hand. This latter kind of variation is expressed by the sampling distribution. Sampling distributions may take many forms and most of those encountered in elementary Statistics have been covered in this book, though there has not been need to introduce their special names. This is a bonus of deriving all such distributions empirically. However, in order to make the link with established terminology we shall briefly rehearse some of the essentials now.

The most important form of sampling distribution is the Normal, and we have seen that this occurs so often because of its link with sums which arise frequently as test statistics. Some examples were given in Chapter 8 where we noted, in particular, that Normality often arose as an approximation when the sample size was large enough. A major area of application was encountered in Chapter 10. There we wished to make inferences about the average but without knowing the variance. An obvious way of dealing with that situation was to replace the unknown variance with an estimate derived from the sample. The resulting sampling distribution looked very similar to a Normal distribution, but we did not need to investigate this matter closely because we derived the sampling distribution from first principles by repeated sampling. However, had we pursued the matter we would have found a systematic departure from the Normal form. The actual sampling distribution has a greater relative frequency in the tails which, of course, pushed the critical values a little farther out than we would have expected if the distribution were really Normal. For largish samples the difference from the Normal does not matter enough to worry about, but with small samples the difference is more important. The name of this sampling distribution is the *t*-distribution. It is associated with the name of W.S. Gossett, better known from his pen-name of 'Student' – in fact, the distribution is often referred to as Student's *t*. Gossett was employed by the Guinness brewery, and it was to keep this link confidential that he was required to use a pen-name. He had close links with Karl Pearson at University College London in whose journal, *Biometrika*, his results were published.

The *t*-distribution arises in other problems, and one of the most important is the comparison of the averages of two samples. There are subtleties here which we do not need to go into, except to point out that the test statistic used is usually defined slightly differently than the one used in this book. This is because the standard treatment brings the statistic into the form required for the use of published tables. There was no need for us to consider such things because of our empirical approach to deriving sampling distributions. The test for comparing the location of two distributions is often known as the two-sample t-test, for obvious reasons.

The forms of the sampling distributions we met in Chapter 11 all showed a family likeness. This was also shared by the sampling distributions of variances in Chapter 9. This similarity is no accident but arises because all these distributions are, in fact, members of the same family known as the *chi-squared distribution*. It typically arises when we are dealing with sums of squares, as we were when testing goodness of fit. The set of distributions constitutes a family whose members differ in shape which is conveniently indicated by their degrees of freedom – which we have linked with the average of the distribution to which it is often equal. Such distributions are skewed, with the degree of skewness determined by the degrees of freedom. As the degrees of freedom become larger so the shape gets closer to the Normal distribution to which it is a good approximation if the degrees of freedom exceed, say, 100.

The remaining distribution, not mentioned so far, is the distribution of the ratio of two variances. This arises especially in the analysis of variance and two examples of the distribution are shown on Figures 10.3 and 10.4. At first sight it looks very much like the chi-squared distribution though it is, in fact, obtained by dividing a variable having one such distribution by another. As in the case of the chi-squared distribution, we are only interested in significance in the upper tail. The usual name for this distribution is the F-distribution. It becomes increasingly like the chi-squared distribution as the number of degrees of freedom of the denominator becomes large, and this means that the whole distribution tends towards Normality if the degrees of freedom in the numerator also become large.

There are two diagrams, Figures 2.4 and 12.5, which go somewhat beyond the text which they are designed to illustrate. Both were constructed using results which are very easy to obtain theoretically but somewhat complicated to derive by simulation. In the case of Figure 12.5, the goodness-of-fit test in the case of a 2 × 2 table is equivalent to basing the test on a single cell frequency whose distribution happens to be known and which is available in R. As the results are for illustration only, this facility has been used to shorten the calculations.

Chapter 13 is concerned, not with new topics, but with the important applications of ideas given earlier in the book. These include the subject of latent, or unobserved, variables, and the example we have taken is intelligence. Although this is not, in some ways, typical of the latent variables which arise in social science it has the merit of being widely known and frequently debated. A book-length treatment of the same topic, also non-mathematical, is given in the author's *Measuring Intelligence: Facts and Fallacies* (Cambridge University Press, 2004). There is an enormous literature on estimating the relationships among latent variables, but all of this lies far outside the boundaries of the present book.

Further Reading

The drive for greater numeracy is unrelenting. At the everyday level, numbers impinge on our thinking, and not least on our purchasing behaviour and general welfare. There have been many attempts to engage the interest of a very wide range of people, partly through books, and to remove some of the mystique which surrounds numeracy. In so far as Statistics is the science of extracting meaning from numbers, it is important that its main ideas should be widely understood.

What is true in general is even more true of social science. The reader of this book will therefore profit from dipping into this field for a broader perspective on the subject of Statistics.

The long-time classic, which still merits attention, is *How to Lie with Statistics* by Darrell Huff. This was originally written in 1954 and became one of the bestselling Statistics books ever. It is still available (Penguin, 1991).

More recently there is *Thinking Statistically* by Uri Bram (2nd edition, Kuri Books, 2012).The author's 'second hope' for the book is that 'the book will be useful for people taking traditional Statistics courses'. The book is very brief and does contain some mathematics. Some may find its use of American English obscure – it certainly helps to know what is meant by a 'grade point average'. Nevertheless, beneath it all there is much of importance and relevance for social science students.

Among the best contemporary books designed to equip the reader for life in a number-based society are *The Tiger That Isn't: Seeing through a*

World of Numbers by Michael Blastland and Andrew Dilnot (new edition, Profile Books, 2008) and *Naked Statistics* by Charles Wheelan (W.W. Norton, 2013). The former book contains a useful guide to 'further reading' and the latter includes many useful references.

The reader who takes the subject further will undoubtedly need to come to grips with probability and risk, and an excellent preparation for that journey is *The Norm Chronicles: Stories and Numbers about Risk* by Michael Blastland and David Spiegelhalter (Profile Books, 2014).

The nearest treatment to the present book, though somewhat different in style and now rather old, is *Statistics without Tears: An Introduction for Non-mathematicians* by Derek Rowntree (Penguin, 2000).

APPENDIX

All of the figures in this book were prepared using the R language. It is not necessary to know anything about this language, or computer programming, to derive full benefit from the book. This appendix is for those readers who are curious about what was involved in preparing the figures or who wish to repeat or vary the calculations which have been made. There are many other languages available which could have been used for this purpose. The figures in the early part of this book were also produced in Excel, which is very widely available in Microsoft Office. Nevertheless, it soon became apparent that the versatility and easy availability of R made it ideal for my purposes. R is easily available and may be downloaded free of charge from the web site www.r-project.org. Another virtue of R for the beginner is that the user does not have to be at ease with mathematical notation to make a start. In order to illustrate these remarks we show how R can be used to reproduce some of the analyses which lie behind some of the figures in this book.

We started with some data collected by counting the number of words in successive sentences of a leading article in the *Times* newspaper – the Times(1) data. The numbers in question were: 4, 9, 10, 10, 15, 15, 16, 17, 17, 19, 19, 21, 21, 22, 22, 23, 27, 29, 30, 31, 33, 33, 33, 35, 35, 38, 41. In order to treat these numbers as a set of data to be analysed they are enclosed in brackets prefixed by 'c' and given a name:

```
data=c(4, 9, 10, 10, 15, 15, 16, 17, 17, 19, 19, 21, 21, 22, 22, 23, 27,
29, 30, 31, 33, 33, 33, 35, 35, 38, 41)
```

We can now do various things with these numbers such as find their average or construct a histogram. To find the average we simply write 'mean(data)' (the word 'mean' is used rather than 'average' because that is what the writers of the language decided).

We have made great use of histograms in this book, and this is achieved in R by the instruction 'hist(data)'. There are all kinds of refinements which can be added inside the brackets to this simple statement. These can be used to give the figure a title, label the axes and so on. In default of such refinements, R will do what it thinks best. (R obviously cannot 'think', but those who worked on the project certainly could, and they provided instructions which are applied in the absence of any provided by the user.)

Figure 1.2 was produced by the following program:

```
#Figure 1.2 Histogram of sentence length frequency for Times(1) data

x=c(27, 23, 33, 15, 21, 38, 16, 15, 4, 19, 21, 9, 33, 41, 10, 30, 35, 19, 17, 31, 33, 17, 22, 10, 22, 29, 35)

hist(x, xlab="Words per sentence", main = "Figure 1.2 Histogram of sentence length frequency for Times(1) data", xlim=c(0,50) )
```

The sentence after the '#' sign is not part of the program and is there merely to remind the user what the program does. For brevity 'x' is used here instead of 'data' and the expressions following 'x' in the hist statement illustrate our remark about refinements which may be included. Thus the title is given after 'main=' and the label 'Words per sentence' is added as the label of the horizontal axis. The final instruction sets a limit for the horizontal scale because all sentence lengths are all less than 50 words.

Some other diagrams can be produced by a single statement, and one such example is the boxplot used in Figure 1.12. This was produced for the same set of data by the program:

```
#Figure 1.12 Boxplot for Times(1) data

x=c(27, 23, 33, 15, 21, 38, 16, 15, 4, 19, 21, 9, 33, 41, 10, 30, 35, 19, 17, 31, 33, 17, 22, 10, 22, 29, 35)

boxplot(x, ylab = "sentence length", main = "Figure 1.12 Boxplot for Times(1) data" )
```

Here also the figure title and the label of the horizontal axis are given in exactly the same way as for the histogram.

The frequency curves for common distributions can be drawn very easily. Actually, R plots the height of the curve, but an illusion of continuity can be obtained by plotting the points very close together. A Normal distribution, such as that in Figure 3.9, is obtained from the following program:

```
#Normal curve N(0,100) Figure 3.9

x=seq(-300,300, by=.1)

y=dnorm(x,0,100)

plot(x,y,type="l",main="Figure 3.9 A Normal distribution", ylab="")
```

The points to be plotted are given by the 'dnorm' instruction, which also specifies the average and variance of the Normal distribution to be drawn. The statement beginning 'x=' ensures that the calculation is made at every point between −300 and +300 at intervals of 0.1. Although this requires calculations to be made for about 6000 points, this is done so rapidly that it is hardly noticeable.

Once the essentials of the diagram have been determined, other features can be added. This is illustrated by Figure 4.1 where vertical lines have been added to a Normal distribution to mark the bounds within which specified proportions of the distribution lie.

Sampling distributions are a constant feature of the book from Chapter 9 onwards. These require, first of all, a large number of samples to be drawn from a specified distribution and then for the frequency distribution to be determined. There is a common feature of all these programs, the essence of which can be expressed by looking at the program which created Figure 10.1. This is as follows:

```
#Figure 10.1 Sampling distribution of t.

b=seq(-8,8, by=.2)

n=10

x=replicate(100000, rnorm(n, 0,1)) #100000 samples of size 10

t=function(x) {mean(x)/sd(x)}

td=apply(x, MARGIN=2, t)

td=td*sqrt(n/(n-1))

td=td*sqrt(n)

hist(td, b,xlab="test statistic", main=("Figure 10.1 Sampling distribution
of test statistic for test on a single mean"))

var(td)

sd(td)
```

We pass over the details of this program but draw attention to the features which are common to all our programs for deriving sampling distributions. The third line, as the comment shows, draws 100,000 samples of size 10 from a standard Normal distribution. The program then calculates the test statistic for each of these samples and stores them in a convenient location until we come to compile their frequency distribution (the sampling distribution in this case).

It is perfectly possible to plot several histograms on the same diagram as in Figures 9.1–9.3. This is achieved by a command which creates several panels inside which the relevant histograms are drawn. Up to nine such panels can be created in three rows and three columns. This enables comparisons to be made visually across rows and columns as in Figure 11.1.

Programs like this make it easily possible to construct sampling distributions for any statistic whatsoever under a very wide range of underlying distributional assumptions – far beyond what is provided for by existing theory. When this is linked to the speed with which these operations can be conducted on even modest home computers, the possibilities opened up are truly impressive.

INDEX

Note: Tables and Figures are indicated by page numbers in bold print.

arithmetic 2
averages 4, 9–10, 48–9, 158
  and dispersion 50, 51, 59
  and location of distributions 57, 58
  and normal distribution **53–4**
  sampling distribution of 99–103, **100, 101, 102**
  and variance 51
  see also inference about averages

bar diagrams 36–7
Bartholomew, David J.: *Measuring Intelligence: Facts and Fallacies* 164
Bayesian methods 161
bell curves **43–4**, 152
between-groups sum of squares (BGSS) 66
binary data 123–34
  binomial distributions 124–6
  durations 130–**1**
  negative binomial distributions 130–1
  Poisson distributions 123, 127, 128
  rare events 127–30, **128**
  relationships 132–4
  two binary variables **133, 134**
  two by two table **132**
Binet, Alfred 149
binomial distributions 124–**6**
Biometrika 8, 162
bivariate data 69–70
Blastland, Michael and Dilnot, Andrew: *The Tiger That Isn't* 164–5
Blastland, Michael and Spiegelhalter, David: *The Norm Chronicles* 165
'bonds model' 149
Bowley, Sir Arthur: *Elements of Statistics* 8
boxplots **21**
Bram, Uri: *Thinking Statistically* 164

calculations 159
causation and correlation 76
central limit theorem 44, 87
chi-squared distribution 163

component distributions 25, 26
computers 159
conditional distributions 74
correlation 74–7
  and causation 76
  spurious correlations 76–7, 148–9
correlation coefficient 75
counts 4–5
covariance structure analysis 156
covariation 10, 69–79
  and correlation 74–7
  inheritance of height from fathers to sons **72, 73**–4
  number of letters per sentence: dot diagrams **71**
  principle of least squares 77–9

Darwin, Charles: *Origin of Species* 7
decomposition 55–67
  analysis of variance 64–7
  comparison of income in six cities 59–63, 66–7
    comparison of travel distances 62–**3**, 67
    dot diagram **60**, 66
    locations and average income **61**, 67
  comparison of two diets 57–9, 62, 65–6
    dot diagram: reduction in weight **58**, 64
  variation in intelligence 155
decreasing frequencies 38
deviations 50, 51
differences 52
discrete distributions 36
dispersion 50–2, 74, **100, 101**, 158
distribution-free tests 120
duration/waiting times 38–9, 130–**1**

emotional intelligence 152
Excel 167
exponential distributions 37–41, **38**
  added variables 40–**1**
  decreasing frequencies 38

exponential distributions *cont.*
  duration/waiting times 38–9
  mixed exponentials 39–**40**

F-distribution 163
first-order interactions 62
Fisher, Sir Ronald 93, 139
frequencies **11**, **19**
  cumulative frequency distribution **20**
frequency curves 19–20, 25–6
frequency distributions 12–20
  cumulative frequency distributions **20**–1
  and sampling distributions 98–9
frequency polygons 20

g-factor 149
Galton, Sir Francis: *Natural Inheritance*
  72, 73
Gaussian distribution 45
  see also normal distribution
goodness of fit 135–45, 163
  2 X 2 table 163
  discrete distribution 144–5
  frequency distribution of 200 random
    numbers **136**
  normal distributions 141–4, **142**
  sampling distribution 138–9
    number of categories and sample size
      140, 141
  two by two table 144–5
Gossett, W.S. 162

higher-order interactions 62
histograms 12–20
  circle sizes between sycamore seedlings **30**
  intervals between vehicles **19**
  nearest neighbour distances of seedlings **16**
  random numbers between 0 and 99 **18**
  random numbers between 0 and 100 **17**
  sentence length frequency **12**
  sentence length frequency (2) **13**
  spam **15**
  time intervals between passing vehicles **15**
Huff, Darrell: *How to Lie with Statistics* 164
hypotheses 97, 121
  null hypotheses 121
  testing 92, 105–6, 107

inference 89–96, 97–109, 159, 160–1
  confidence coefficients 96
  confidence intervals **95**–6
  estimate of variance 106–7
  estimation 107
  hypothesis testing 105–6, 107

inference *cont.*
  P-value (significance level) 92
  sampling distributions
    of the average 99–103, **100**, **101**,
      102, 106
    determination of 105
    non-normal 108–9
    of the variance 103–5, **104**, 108–9
  value of distance from average 92–3
  and value of variables 90–1
inference about averages 111–22
  assumptions 119
  more than two samples 116–18
    between-groups variance 117
    test statistic **116**–17
  power 121–2, 161
  from a single sample 112
    test statistic **113**
  from two samples 115–16
intelligence 147, 148–9
  nature versus nurture debate 147, 154–5
  types of intelligence 152, 153
intelligence testing 149–51
  cultural bias 151, 152
  domain 151–2
  one- and two- dimensions 153–4
  scores 151–2
interactions 61, 62
interpreting variation 23–34
  adding and differencing 26–30, **28**, **29**
  combined distributions 24–6, **25**
  logarithmic transformations of
    duration **34**
  transformations 30–4, **31**, **32**
    duration **33**
    rescaling **32**
interval estimates 107
  attaching a probability 107

kurtosis 54

Laplace, Pierre Simon de 8
latent variables *see* unobserved variables
location 95, 99, 163
  and average 49, 57, 58
  and dispersion 50
  measures of 47, 48–9, 158
  shifts in **31**, **32**, **33**, **34**

marginal distributions 73
mathematics in statistics 1–3
means 158
  see also averages
measurement error 45

measurements 3, 4–7
  instruments 5
  levels 6
  measurement error 45
  ordinal 6
  scales 5–6
  units 5–6
memorylessness of exponential
    distribution 39
Mendel, Gregor 139

non-normal sampling distributions
    108–9
normal distributions 42–5, 53–4, 162
  bell curve **43–4, 90**
  dot diagram **42**
  goodness of fit 141–4, **143**
  histograms 43
  normalising tendency 44
  standard normal distribution **53**
  and values of variables **90–1**
null hypotheses 121
numbers 3–4

one- and two-tailed tests 93, 115–16
ordinal numbers 4
origins of statistics 7–8
overdispersion 130

parameters 161
patterns 12, 17, 19
Pearson, Karl 7, 8, 51, 162
picturing variation 10–21
  boxplots 21
  cumulative frequency distribution
    20–1
  frequency curves 19–20
  frequency polygons 20
  histograms 12–20
  scales 11–12, **13**
point estimation 107
Poisson distributions 123, 127, 128
populations 82
power 121–**2**, 161
principle of least squares 77–9
  predicting number of letters from number
    of words **78, 79**
probability sampling 89

R language 167–70
random numbers 135–6
randomness: frequency distribution table
    136–7
  goodness of fit calculation **138**

rare events 127–30
  for various averages **128**
rectangular distributions 36, 37
regression lines 78–9
robust procedures 119
Rowntree, Derek: *Statistics without Tears* 165

sampling 81–7
  bias 82–3
  cluster sampling 86
  from an infinite population 87
  and populations 82
  probability sampling 89
  quota sampling 85
  sample size 108
  sampling without replacement 84
  simple random sampling 83–4
  stratified random sampling 85–6
  transformation 87
  see also inference
sampling distributions 98–9, 159, 160, 162
  of the average 99–103, **100, 101, 102,** 106
  determination of 105
  of goodness of fit 138–**9**
  non-normal 108–9
  standard error 98, 102–3
  of the variance 103–5, **104,** 108–9
scales **11, 13**
significance tests 159–60
skewness 54
social variability 45
Spearman, Charles 148–9
spurious correlations 76–7, 148–9
standard deviation 51, 104, 158
standard distributions 35–45
  exponential distribution 37–41
  normal distribution 42–5
  uniform distribution 36–7
standard error 98, 102–3, 112, **113,** 114, 121
'statistic': definition 98
statistical models 79
statistical tables 159
Stigler, S.M. 7
Student's *t* 162
stylometrics 23
summarising variation 47–54
survival curves 21

t-distribution 162–3
temperature 5–6
Terman, Lewis 149
testing 149–50
  calibration 150
  hypotheses 92

Thomson, Godfrey 149
total sum of squares (TSS) 66
transformations 30–4, 31, 32, 44–5
two by two table 132, 144–5
Type I error probability 92

uncertainty 10, 161
uniform distributions 18, 36–7
unobserved variables 147–56
    index approach 149–54
    in social science 155–6
    spurious correlation approach 148–9, 152

variables: definition 5
variance 51–2, 64–7
variance ratio 117, 163
variation 4, 7
    and averages 9–10
    decomposition of 55–67, 155, 158
    identifying sources of 157–8
    interpreting 23–34
    picturing 10–21
    summarising 47–54

within-groups sum of squares (WGSS) 66